KEYS TO CURRENT EN

Volume I

Mildred Brocklehurst

CEC

CENTRE ÉDUCATIF ET CULTUREL INC.
8101, boul. Métropolitain Est, Anjou, Qc, Canada. H1J 1J9
Téléphone: (514) 351-6010   Télécopie: (514) 351-3534

Project editor, copy editor: **Jonathan Paterson**
Managing director, ESL: **Leena M. Sandblom**
Production manager: **Lucie Plante-Audy**
Art direction and page design: **Maurice Paradis,** Productions Fréchette et Paradis
Illustrations: **Dan Allen**
Cover illustration and design: **Michel Allard**

Credits
Page 6: photographs by Kéro (left) and André Le Coz (right) reproduced with the permission of Kim Yaroshevskaya
Page 9: photographs: Corel Corporation
Page 15: photograph: Dan Allen
Pages 27–28: "The Price of Perfection" reprinted with permission—The Toronto Star Syndicate.
Page 34: photograph reproduced with the permission of Andrew Golding
Pages 48–49: "Morale Booster" reproduced with the permission of Bee MacGuire
Page 49: Photo: Créations Earthrise inc.
Page 57: photograph reproduced with the permission of Don Koszukan
Pages 66–67: Script for "Growing Food in the City": Developing Countries Farm Radio Network, Toronto, Canada
Pages 72–73: "Alberta Sisters are Entrepreneurial Winners" reproduced with the permission of The Canadian Press.
Pages 77–78: photographs: Corel Corporation
Page 80: top and bottom photographs reproduced with the permission of Dr. Lee Boyd: middle photograph: Corel Corporation; interview recording reproduced with the permission of the Canadian Broadcasting Corporation
Pages 93–94: "A `Tree Hugger' Recycles Fur" reproduced with the permission of the International Herald Tribune
Page 99: photograph: Corel Corporation
Page 102: photograph: Sue Lea
Pages 117–118: "On-Board Computers Mean End of the Car as We Know It, Honda's Chief Engineer Says" reproduced with the permission of the Windsor Star
Page 129: photograph reproduced with the permission of Claire Rothman
Pages 145–146: Introduction from *Shifting Gears: Thriving in the New Economy* by Nuala Beck. Copyright © 1992. Published by HarperCollins Publishers Ltd

© 1995, Centre Éducatif et Culturel inc.
8101, boul. Métropolitain Est
Anjou, Québec   H1J 1J9

Dépôt légal, Bibliothèque nationale du Québec, 1er trimestre 1995
Legal deposit, National Library of Canada, 1st quarter 1995

ISBN 2-7617-1137-8

Printed in Canada

Introduction

Who This Book Is For

Keys to Current English, Volume I, is for students of English at a middle or intermediate level.

What This Book Consists Of

Keys to Current English, Volume I, contains six units organized around general themes. In each unit, there are three readings with associated speaking and writing activities, grammar reviews, vocabulary study and listening comprehension assignments.

The grammar reviews include the parts of speech, with special emphasis on verb forms.

The writing exercises are designed to enable students to produce, with ease and fluency, compositions in which they use the grammar and vocabulary they are studying.

The speaking activities are also structured to present occasions to put into practice what is being studied and to generate spontaneous responses in the course of debates, discussions, pair work and group work.

The listening component of *Keys to Current English, Volume I,* provides opportunities to acquire comprehension skills in this important area of language study.

How This Book Can Help You

The activities and exercises in *Keys to Current English, Volume I,* are designed to assist you as you continue to develop the four language skills—listening, speaking, reading and writing—so that you will use English with more confidence, speak and write with greater ease and accuracy, and not be afraid to make mistakes, but will be able to correct them yourself and to learn from them.

Good luck with your studies!

Acknowledgments

Grateful acknowledgments to Elaine Breault of Cégep Ahuntsic, Edna Downey of Cégep de Saint-Jérôme, Karen Gilbert of Cégep Saint-Jean-sur-Richelieu, Margaret Gregory of Cégep Ahuntsic, Ian Mason of Cégep de Jonquière and David Strickland of Cégep François-Xavier-Garneau, whose generous contributions of their time, experience and knowledge in commenting on parts of the manuscript were of enormous benefit.

Special thanks to David Cranson of Cégep de Saint-Laurent, Jonathan Paterson, and Leena M. Sandblom of CEC. Their recommendations and suggestions were invaluable in maintaining the focus of this endeavour.

And finally a word of thanks for the encouragement and support of all who participated in the realization of the project at CEC.

Contents

Identities

In this unit, you are going to read about names and faces—two of the things we use to identify ourselves and others. You will do a writing assignment based on one of the texts, as well as related listening-comprehension exercises and oral activities integrated with the unit theme. You will also work on certain aspects of grammar—the parts of speech—with particular emphasis on nouns and pronouns.

Overview

Focus on Names

Your name can refer both to your *personal name* or *given name* and to the combination of your personal name and your *family name,* also known as *your surname.*

A nickname is a name used instead of your real name. For example, if your name is Caroline and everybody calls you Caro, that's your nickname. Or if your name is Bernard, you have red hair, and everyone calls you Red instead of Bernard, Red is your nickname.

Now that you know something about names, see if you can find someone in the class who

Your Classmate's Name

1. has a nickname. What is it?

2. has the same name as a parent or grandparent.

3. has the same surname as a famous person.

4. has a name beginning with one of these letters: B J M R Y.

5. knows what an alias is.

Names

Getting the Point

Skim the text on pages 3–4 by looking at the title and illustration, and reading the first sentence of each paragraph. Then answer this question.

This text is about

a) how people get their nicknames.

b) roses.

c) cars.

d) how people are influenced by names.

Now read the whole text to confirm your prediction.

Did you get it right? Now that you've got the topic, find the answers to Getting the Details, page 4.

Names

"What's in a name?" asked Shakespeare, adding that a rose with any other name would still be a rose and would still smell sweet. He was right; giving something a name doesn't change its true nature, but—and this is a big qualification—we can be and frequently are influenced by names.

This is not news in the business world, where naming products to sell to consumers is taken very seriously. Sometimes the name is a pure fabrication, with no particular connection to the merchandise itself. Kodak comes to mind as an example of this type of name. On the other hand, the chosen name could be associated with the product's function, as in the case of Frigidaire. Just think of the names of many of the items you use daily and try to imagine how the selection process unfolded. Who decided that Bold is good for a laundry detergent or Oasis for fruit juice?

Better still, take the names given to cars. Often they suggest animals known for their strength, swiftness and wild beauty. It would never occur to an expert in marketing to call a car an elephant, a whale or a hippopotamus. The rea-sons are obvious. These creatures are slow-moving and ponderous. They might be lovable, but they do not create a mental picture of streamlined speed and so they are automatically disqualified.

When the list of acceptable animals is exhausted, associations with well-known, glamorous and exciting places are selected, and after that slightly mysterious and classical-sounding words like Acura, Integra, Lexus and Cygna come into play. The motivation behind the selection remains unchanged: the name chosen should evoke positive images—whether it is the designation of something that exists or a construction created by an advertising agency.

A recent experiment with the naming of a French car demonstrates just how important it is to make the right choices. A large car manufacturer had a new product to launch on the market—a small-sized vehicle designed exclusively for city use, with low fuel consumption, ease of parking and numerous other features developed specifically to appeal to the urban dweller.

But something was missing, and that something was a good name. The manufacturer wanted one that would be simple, easy to remember and original, and gave the job of finding it to a team famous for using computers to solve problems.

What did the computer team eventually produce as an appropriate name? Twingo! Yes, Twingo. You read it correctly.

The team did everything it was asked to do: it

produced a name that was simple, easy to remember and original, but it just wasn't good enough. Why not?

The missing element was context, an association that means something. Psychologists refer to this as cognitive resonance. When a new article like a camera or an electric refrigerator makes its appearance, it doesn't matter too much if the name lacks cognitive resonance. This will develop eventually as the product and name become known.

This was not the case with Twingo. Cars are not an unknown quantity, so a new name for a new car should contain some element of cognitive resonance. It just wasn't there, so the response of the test group evaluating Twingo as a name was negative.

Twingo was just a meaningless string of letters. It created no images in the minds of those who heard it; as a name, Twingo was equivalent to zero. In brief, Twingo was a gigantic flop.

Which brings us back to Shakespeare's question, "What's in a name?" A great deal more, it appears, than most of us realize—and, as the Twingo episode illustrates, much more than a computer can appreciate. ✍

Getting the Details

Circle the letter that corresponds to what you read in the text "Names". Find the lines in the article that support your choice and note the line numbers.

1 "What's in a name?" was the question posed by
   a) a French car manufacturer.
   b) an expert in marketing.
   c) a computer team.
   d) Shakespeare.

   Line(s)

2 Giving something a name
   a) doesn't change its true nature.
   b) can be done by the manufacturer of a product.
   c) can be done by a computer team.
   d) all of the above

   Line(s)

3 Naming products to sell to consumers
   a) should be taken seriously.
   b) should be done by computers.
   c) would never occur to an expert in marketing.
   d) should never be done by advertising agencies.

   Line(s)

4 Cars are not named after whales and elephants because these creatures are
   a) slightly mysterious and their names sound too classical.
   b) known for their strength, swiftness and wild beauty.
   c) lovable.
   d) slow-moving and ponderous.

   Line(s)

5 The car manufacturers were looking for a name that would be
   a) simple.
   b) easy to understand.
   c) original.
   d) all of the above

   Line(s)

6 The name Twingo
   a) created positive images in the minds of the test group.
   b) was the name chosen for a computer.
   c) was a meaningless string of letters.
   d) means easy to park.

   Line(s)

4

7 Context is an association that
   a) remains unchanged.
   b) means something.
   c) should be simple, easy to remember and original.
   d) is negative.

   Line(s)

8 Psychologists use the term "cognitive resonance" to mean
   a) a computer program.
   b) evoking positive images.
   c) an association that means something.
   d) a flop.

   Line(s)

9 Twingo was not a success because
   a) it was not the name of an exciting place.
   b) it created no images in the minds of those who heard it.
   c) it was not a good name for a rose.
   d) it was not the name of a lovable animal.

   Line(s)

Family Names

Family names are interesting because some of the practices for creating them are common to many different cultures.
Maybe you can find examples in the class for these origins:

Origin

An occupation

A physical characteristic

Ancestry

A geographical location

Examples

Baker, _____

Short, _____

Davidson, _____

Forest, _____

See if you find any other origins for family names among your classmates and add them to the list.

_____   _____

_____   _____

_____   _____

If you really want to find out more about names—your own name, for example—try the dictionary section of your library. It probably has at least one reference work on personal names.

5

Interview
with Kim Yaroshevskaya

Here you see three letters in the Russian alphabet. They spell the name Kim.

КИМ

Kim Yaroshevskaya

Kim as Fanfreluche

The person you are going to hear, Kim Yaroshevskaya, is an actress whose work in both French and English is familiar to television and theatre audiences. She is also the creator of Fanfreluche, one of the most famous imaginary characters in television programs for young people.

6

Getting the Point

Listen to the recording a first time to find the answers to these questions.

		Yes	No
1.	Did Kim like her first name when she was a little girl?	◯	◯
2.	Did she like it when she came to Canada?	◯	◯
3.	Did she like it when she was 18?	◯	◯

Getting the Details

Listen to the recording again to find the answers to these questions.

1 In Russia, Kim was
- *a)* a unisex name.
- *b)* mostly a girls' name.
- *c)* mostly a boys' name.
- *d)* only a boys' name.

2 Kim's parents were both
- *a)* anarchists.
- *b)* Trotskyists.
- *c)* not interested in politics.
- *d)* very interested in politics.

3 Which of these three Russian words means "of youth"?
- *a)* Интернационал
- *b)* Коммунистический
- *c)* Молодежи

4 After she moved to Montreal, Kim wanted to be called
- *a)* Gladys.
- *b)* Natasha.
- *c)* Thelma
- *d)* Lisa.

5 At school, Kim had to change her family name because
- *a)* the other students thought her name was funny.
- *b)* the citizenship judge made a mistake.
- *c)* the principal couldn't pronounce Yaroshevskaya.
- *d)* the principal thought her name was too difficult.

6 Kim got her name back when she
- *a)* got her high-school diploma.
- *b)* became a Canadian citizen.
- *c)* stopped living with her aunt and uncle.
- *d)* began to work as an actress.

Basic Punctuation

Before you do the writing assignment on page 9, you might want to review some important points about the use of punctuation and capital letters.

Punctuation Mark	Use	Examples
Period (.)	Ends an affirmative or negative sentence	It's warm today. It isn't warm today.
Question mark (?)	Ends a direct question.	Is it warm today?
Exclamation mark (!)	Indicates emotion or surprise.	It's so warm today!
Comma (,)	Separates two equal parts of a sentence.	I know the names of the days of the week, and I know you write them with a capital letter.
	Separates words in a series.	We took tomatoes, lettuce, celery, eggs and ham with us for the picnic.

Uses of Capital Letters	Examples
The first word in a sentence	You have to write the names of the days and months with a capital letter.
The first-person singular pronoun, I	Mary and I are in the same class.
All proper nouns (specific names given to people, animals, places and things)	**People:** Charles, Martin, Suzanne, Lucy **Animals:** Rover, Tabby, Whisky **Places:** Mexico, Africa, Rouyn, Gaspé **Things:** Mona Lisa (a painting), The Kiss (a sculpture)
Adjectives derived from proper nouns	American, Japanese, Italian, French, Spanish We all like Italian food.
The days of the week and the months	Monday, September

Writing about Names

Writing

Choose three or four interesting names in one category. They could be names of people, places, movies, rock groups or brand names for a specific category of products, for example.

Decide why you think these names are interesting. Are the reasons different for different names? Make a list of all the reasons you have found. Then compare notes with your classmates.

Using your notes as a guide, write a composition explaining what kinds of names appeal to you. Include three or four examples.

Your composition should be about five to ten sentences long.

_____

_____

_____

_____

_____

_____

_____

_____

Talking about Names

Recently a successful Quebec writer, Marc Poissant, signed a contract with a large American publishing company. Under the terms of the deal, the name on the books to be published in English will be Mark Fisher!

Marc Poissant agreed to the name change for the American market.

That's strange, considering that a recent literary prize winner was Annie Proulx, an American with Quebec roots. No one complained about her name. And everyone seems to be able to pronounce it correctly. Céline Dion doesn't seem to have a problem either.

Was Marc Poissant right to change his name to Mark Fisher?

Express your opinion and see how the class feels about this. Is the class for or against Marc Poissant's decision?

9

The Parts of Speech

We've been reading about, writing about and discussing names. The different kinds of words we use to express ourselves have names, too. These *parts of speech* are: nouns, pronouns, verbs, adjectives, adverbs, prepositions, conjunctions and interjections.

As you study grammar, you will often meet these terms. It is particularly useful to know and understand them, for example, when you use a dictionary.

One good reason for this is that the same form can often have multiple functions and meanings. Take a simple word like *walk*. You probably know it as a verb. It's used that way in the sentence "I usually *walk* to work." But it can also be a noun, as in "They go for a *walk* every day." Knowing how to recognize and define verbs, nouns, etc., and their functions will help you in your grammar studies.

Part of Speech	Function	Examples
Nouns	Identify people, animals, places, things and ideas.	**People:** brother, Mary Martin **Animals:** cows, elephant **Places:** city, Vancouver **Things:** book, car, carrot, pencils **Ideas:** beauty, liberty
Pronouns	Substitute for or replace nouns.	brother → he, him Mary Martin → she, her city → it Vancouver → it book, car, carrot → it pencils → they, them beauty, liberty → it
Verbs	Indicate actions or states.	**Action:** Charles **walks** to work every day. They **walk** to work every day. **State:** Charles always **feels** good after a walk. They always **feel** good after a walk.
Adjectives	Describe nouns.	That **green** book is on the **big** table.
Adverbs	Modify verbs, adjectives and other adverbs.	**Verbs:** Mary always answers questions **quickly**. **Adjective:** The children are **very** good. **Adverbs:** Mary answered that question **quite** quickly.

Prepositions	Show the relationships between words.	Charles begins work every day **at** eight o'clock. There is a bus stop **across** the street. The bus goes **to** the Metro station.
Conjunctions	Connect words or parts of sentences to each other.	Tom **and** Jerry are two cartoon characters. They bought sandwiches for the picnic, **but** they forgot to buy drinks. The bus service operates between eight **and** ten every morning.
Interjections	Show emotion.	**Oh!** We almost forgot!

In addition to the eight traditional parts of speech, it is useful to consider determiners as a separate class. The determiners include the articles *the* and *a/an*, the demonstratives *this* and *that*, and the indefinites *some* and *any*. Most determiners, but not the articles, can also be used as pronouns.

Determiners	Function	Examples
the *this/these* *that/those*	Indicate that a noun is specific.	**The** milk in the refrigerator is sour. **The** students are ready. **This** cat is very friendly. I borrowed **these** books from the library. **That** colour is pretty. Do you like **those** houses?
a/an *some* *any*	Indicate that a noun is not specific.	**A** cat meowed. **An** apple every day is good for you. **Some** cats like mushroom soup. They bought **some** sandwiches. He didn't have **any** bus tickets.

Applying the Rules

Examine these sentences taken from the text on pages 3–4, and identify the part of speech of each word in bold print.

1. **He** was **right;** giving something **a name** doesn't change its **true nature, but** we **can be** and **frequently** are influenced **by** names. *(lines 3–7)*

Word	Part of Speech	Word	Part of Speech
He	pronoun	nature	
right	adjective	but	
a	determiner	can be	
name		frequently	
true		by	

2. **They are automatically** disqualified. *(lines 33–34)*

They		automatically	
are			

3. **Associations with** well-known, **glamorous and exciting** places are selected, and **after that slightly** mysterious and classical-sounding words. *(lines 36–40)*

Associations		exciting	
with		after	
glamorous		that	
and		slightly	

4. **The motivation behind** the selection **remains** unchanged. *(lines 42–43)*

The		behind	
motivation		remains	

Talking about Faces

How do we respond to people's faces? Look at this series of photographs and decide which faces you find most attractive.

Try to describe each of the faces. Is there a common element in the faces you find most attractive? What makes some faces more attractive than others?

13

Is Beauty Cultural?

Getting the Point

Skim the text on pages 15–16 by looking only at the title, the headings, and the first and last paragraphs. What is the main idea in the text?

a) Physical beauty is culturally determined.

b) Large eyes, high cheekbones, full lips and narrow chins are attractive.

c) Some scientists think that there are universal elements of beauty.

d) Nature makes babies cute to motivate their parents to protect them.

Now read the whole text to confirm your prediction. Did you get it right?

Now that you've got the main idea, find the answers to Getting the Details.

Getting the Details

Indicate whether each of the following statements (a) agrees with the text, (b) disagrees with the text, or (c) does not correspond to anything in the text. If your answer is (a) or (b), identify the lines in the text that support your choice.

1 Most people have always thought that standards of beauty are culturally determined. [Line(s)]

2 The British/Japanese study was specifically designed to challenge traditional assumptions. [Line(s)]

3 The faces considered attractive by the Japanese and British participants all had full lips. [Line(s)]

4 Dr. Langlois suggests that there are several different standards of beauty. [Line(s)]

5 Dr. Langlois proposes survival as the reason why young mammals are cute. [Line(s)]

6 The author thinks the conclusions of the two studies are probably valid. [Line(s)]

Is BEAUTY Cultural?

FROM OUR SCIENCE
CORRESPONDENT

Is physical beauty something that is culturally determined?

For centuries, it was assumed that what
appealed to, say, a Norwegian would not
have the same attractiveness for an
Indonesian and vice versa. Familiarity tri-
umphed and that was that. Period.

There was no reason to
think otherwise—until,
that is, the results of a
recent cross-cultural
study of facial attractiveness were published.
They challenge this
assumption in no uncer-
tain terms and, what's
more, their conclu-
sions are supported by
some other recent
experiments—all of
which seem to show
that universal stan-
dards of beauty
exist.

So perhaps it's worth examining the studies
and seeing what their findings were.

Big Eyes Appealing

The first involved British and Japanese participants, including both men and women.
They rated photographs of faces of both
Caucasians and Asians for attractiveness,
with the astonishing result that the two
groups came up with almost identical assessments.

The Japanese faces that were attractive to the
Japanese were also beautiful to the British,
and the Japanese reacted similarly to the
Caucasian photographs. The same faces were
preferred, regardless of race. The conclusion
to be drawn? Racial characteristics were
decidedly not a determining factor.

But this is the truly interesting phenomenon:
the attractive faces all had certain things in
common—big eyes, high cheekbones, full
lips and a narrow chin—and these were the
elements that formed the
basis for deciding
whether a face was
appealing or not.

Infant Preferences

That's not all. Dr.
Judith Langlois, a psy-
chologist at the
University of Texas, has
done a similar study to
determine the kinds of
faces that appeal to
babies. Some of the
infants in her investigation
were as young as two
months old, but they still had a preference for
the same kinds of faces as those described in
the British-Japanese study.

Dr. Langlois says her experiment questions
the conventional wisdom that notions of
physical attractiveness are culturally determined. Indeed she suggests that our preference for a certain facial geometry may have
evolved over the ages of human development
and may be a standard for all races.

large eyes

high cheekbones

full lips

narrow chin

Certainly her research with infants seems to lend support for this view. While some may argue that the Japanese-British experimentation might have been influenced by global dissemination of images of beautiful people of all races, the same cannot be said for Dr. Langlois' sample. Obviously, two-month-old babies have not had this exposure. Yet they too showed the same significant preferences.

Survival of the Cutest

Why should this be so? One proposal is that the favoured face has a certain cuteness common to human infants and the young of many other mammals. The sceptics might shrug their shoulders and say "so what", "big deal" or some other sneering dismissal. Everyone knows, they will contend, that babies, kittens, puppies, infant elephants, etc., are adorable, so what does that prove?

Well, it may not prove anything, but it cer-tainly raises the question of why human babies and other young mammals are cute. In a word, the answer is survival.

The young of homo sapiens and the higher mammals have a long period of dependency on their parents before they can function as autonomous beings. And that, many think, is the reason for the cute baby face. It's purposely designed to arouse feelings of love and protectiveness. It's irresistible. We all respond to it without realizing that it's just another of Mother Nature's mechanisms designed to motivate parents to stay at their job long enough to ensure the baby's safe transition to maturity.

But Mother Nature's legacy seems, according to the work of Dr. Langlois and that of the British-Japanese research team, to have had far-reaching consequences. For it now appears that it has provided us with a universal template for evaluating facial appeal.

Vocabulary in Context

Identify each word in the first column as a noun, a verb, an adjective or an adverb, according to how it used in the text. Then match the word with the most suitable definition.

Words

1. assessments *(line 33)* ___noun___ ___d___

2. astonishing *(line 32)* _____ _____

3. beings *(line 98)* _____ _____

4. challenge *(line 14)* _____ _____

5. cross-cultural *(line 11)* _____ _____

6. homo sapiens *(line 95)* _____ _____

Definitions

a) associated with more than one group of people or nationality

b) conversely; the other way around

c) evaluated

d) evaluations

e) even so, in spite of this

f) humans considered as a species

16

Words	Definitions
7. mammals *(lines 85, 93, 96)* _____ ___	**g)** ideas
8. notions *(line 66)* _____ ___	**h)** members of the class of animals that includes humans
9. participants *(line 28)* _____ ___	**i)** people and animals
10. rated *(line 30)* _____ ___	**j)** people taking part in something
11. still *(line 62)* _____ ___	**k)** question, dispute
12. vice versa *(line 6)* _____ ___	**l)** very surprising

The Barbie Syndrome

The subject of this report is the cultural effect of a very popular toy, the Barbie doll.

Here's some unfamiliar vocabulary you will hear, with explanations about how it is used in the context.

First, the word *syndrome* is in the title. It means a characteristic pattern.

The expression *over the hill* means old, out of date, passé.

Housebound means having to stay in the house.

Phoney means not real, not sincere.

Flawlessness is a synonym for perfection.

Narcissistic means extreme self-admiration, especially physical self-admiration.

Backlash refers to an unexpected negative consequence or reaction.

Subversion, in its true sense, means a secret attempt to destroy a system. It's used figuratively in this report to refer to the unexpected effects Barbie dolls may have.

Long, in this context, is a verb meaning to desire.

Getting the Point

Listen to the report a first time to identify the speaker's main point.

a) Barbie is popular because of feminism.

b) Barbie is a great toy.

c) Barbie is not a good role model to present to little girls.

d) Barbie is a feminist role model.

Getting the Details

Now that you've got the main idea, listen to the report again and try to find the answers to these questions.

1 What age was given for Barbie?

   a) 20

   b) 25

   c) 30

   d) 35

2 At this age Barbie should be considered

   a) no longer popular.

   b) over the hill.

   c) a feminist.

   d) a phoney.

3 Barbie

   a) is as popular now as when she first arrived in North American toy stores.

   b) is a model of plastic perfection.

   c) comes with wigs and wardrobes.

   d) is all of the above.

   e) is none of the above.

4 Talking Barbie was pulled from the market because

   a) she was a symbol of phoney flawlessness.

   b) she proudly proclaimed her ignorance of math.

   c) she was a feminist.

   d) she wasn't interested in shiny floors.

5 Some young women today are literally dying

   a) to have a Barbie doll.

   b) to have incredible opportunities.

   c) to be feminists.

   d) to have the perfect smile.

Nouns and Pronouns

Both nouns and pronouns can be subjects of verbs, objects of verbs and objects of prepositions.

Function	Examples
Subject of a verb	The **participants** rated photographs of faces. **They** rated photographs of faces.
Object of a verb	The researchers observed the **participants**. The researchers observed **them**.
Object of a preposition	Some of the **participants** were Japanese. Some of **them** were Japanese.

Subject and Object Forms

Nouns can be subjects or objects without changes in form. On the other hand, many pronouns change their forms according to their function in a sentence.

Subject	Object	Examples
I	me	I want to improve my English. Please help **me**. Talk to **me** in English.
he	him	He has a nickname. Everybody calls **him** Red.
she	her	She studied infants. The journalist interviewed **her**.
we	us	We received a letter. The letter was delivered to **us**.
they	them	They studied faces. The researchers studied **them**.
who	who/whom*	Who was there? Who did you speak to? To **whom** did you speak?

* Many purists consider that *whom* is the correct object form, but *who* is very widely used.

Singular and Plural

Some pronouns and most nouns have different forms depending on whether they are *singular* (referring to one person or thing) or *plural* (referring to two or more persons or things).

Singular Pronouns	Plural Pronouns
I	we
he, she, it	they
me	us
him, her	them
this	these
that	those

Regular Noun Plurals	Examples
For most nouns, just add *s* to the singular form.	table + s → tables toy + s → toys
If the singular ends in *s, x, z, ch* or *sh*, add *es*. Note: This *es* ending is pronounced as an additional syllable.	loss + es → losses tax + es → taxes quizz + es → quizzes patch + es → patches bush + es → bushes Exception: stomach → stomachs
If the singular ends in a consonant followed by *y*, change the *y* to *i* and then add *es*.	country + es → countries pastry + es → pastries
Oh! Oh!—words ending in *o* are more complicated. Generally, add *es*. Some words ending in *o* (generally words referring to music) just add *s*.	tomato + es → tomatoes alto + s → altos

Irregular Noun Plurals	Examples
Some common English words have irregular plurals.	man → men woman → women child → children person → people **or** persons foot → feet tooth → teeth goose → geese mouse → mice
Some names of animals do not change in form.	sheep → sheep deer → deer moose → moose
Some words ending in an *f* sound have a *v* sound in the plural.	leaf + **es** → leaves life + **s** → lives shelf + **es** → shelves wife + **s** → wives
Words borrowed from other languages often keep the foreign plural form.	**French:** tableau → tableaux **Latin:** crisis → crises **Latin:** addendum → addenda **Greek:** phenomenon → phenomena

Applying the Rules

Practise what you have just studied by completing these exercises.

A. Rewrite the following paragraph, changing the elements in bold print to the correct plural forms.

I often have to spell **my name** when I speak to someone on the telephone. In fact, the **man** who spoke to **me** yesterday about taking **this child** I know to Toronto with **him** asked **me** to repeat the spelling more than once. When I called later to confirm with **him**, the **woman** handling the details said, "Oh! **That name!** How do I spell **it?**" I felt like telling **her** that **her** comments irritated **me**, but **that remark** wouldn't really help.

_____

_____

_____

_____

_____

_____

_____

_____

_____

_____

_____

B. Rewrite the following paragraph, changing the elements in bold print to the correct singular forms.

These friends of **ours** really believed people grow to look like their pets. **They** *(two possibilities)* showed us pictures to prove **their** *(two possibilities)* point. The first picture was of **these men** with dogs with droopy eyes like bloodhounds'. The **men** had eyes just like the dogs'. The other picture was of the **women** at a cat show in Paris. No doubt about it, **they** definitely had a feline look about **them.** It seemed to **us** that **our friends** made **their** *(two possibilities)* point very well.

_____

_____

_____

_____

_____

_____

_____

_____

_____

_____

Possessive Forms

Both nouns and pronouns change their forms to show possession.

Patterns for Possessive Nouns	Examples
If the noun is a plural ending in *s*, add an apostrophe after the *s*.	the students' work
In other cases, add 's.*	Mary's brother the boss's office the children's toys

* Many proper nouns ending in *s* can take either just the apostrophe or 's.

Possessive Forms of Pronouns

There are two kinds of possessive pronoun forms. One goes before a noun and the other stands alone.

Subject	Object	Possessive + Noun	Possessive Alone	Possessive Examples
I	me	my	mine	My name is . . . This is **mine**
you	you	your	yours	Your name is . . . This is **yours.**
he	him	his	his	His name is . . . This is **his.**
she	her	her	hers	Her name is . . . This is **hers.**
it	it	its*	—	Its name is . . .
we	us	our	ours	Our name is . . . This is **ours.**
they	them	their	theirs	Their name is . . . This is **theirs.**
who	who/ whom	whose	whose	Whose name is . . . ? Whose is it?

* Watch out for this possessive. Don't confuse it with the contracted form of *it + is → it's*.

Applying the Rules

You can use the information about possessive forms in these exercises.

A. Complete the sentences with the possessive forms of the nouns in bold print.

1. Today is **Sue** __ birthday.

2. Today is **Charles** __ birthday.

3. Is that your **teacher** __ office?

4. Is that a **student** __ book?

5. Are those the **students** __ books?

B. Circle the correct possessive forms.

1. Charles is **my / mine** friend.

2. **Their / Theirs** house is on the corner.

3. The house on the corner is **their / theirs.**

4. We eat **our / ours** lunch in the cafeteria.

5. It's **your / yours** turn to answer the telephone.

6. It's not **my / mine** turn; it's **her / hers.**

7. Don't sit here; this place is **my / mine.**

8. I didn't have any paper so I took some of **your / yours.**

C. Substitute pronoun forms for the words in bold print in the following text.

A large number of **surnames** describe people's occupations. Margaret Thatcher, a former prime minister of England, has just such a name. **Margaret Thatcher's** surname indicates that ancestors of **Margaret Thatcher's** followed the occupation of thatching, making roofs out of dried grasses. Today there is little demand for **thatchers,** but the name survives even if the craft which produced **the name** is rarely required.

_____

_____

_____

_____

_____

_____

_____

_____

_____

Presenting Faces

Make a group presentation to the class.

Look through some old magazines to find interesting pictures of faces of people or animals. The pictures must be big enough for everyone to see. Each group must present four faces.

In your presentation, show the pictures and describe the faces. Say why you think they are interesting. You may want to compare them to each other.

At the end of your presentation, the rest of the class will be expected to participate by asking questions. Be ready to answer them.

Plan your project so that everyone in the group gives part of the presentation.

Making Faces

Use the examples in the following text to match the idioms with their definitions.

Joan wanted to have a tattoo, but her father was against it. She decided to put on a bold face and *fly in the face* of his opposition. Then she discovered she could get a removable tattoo. That *put a new face* on her problem. The solution was *staring her in the face*. She put on a removable tattoo and went home to *face the music*, but she could hardly *keep a straight face*. Her father's anger was as *plain as the nose on his face*, but she *made a face* and told him it wasn't a real tattoo.

1. face the music   *a*
2. fly in the face of   ___
3. keep a straight face   ___
4. make a face   ___
5. as plain as the nose on one's face   ___
6. put a new face on   ___
7. put on a bold face   ___
8. staring someone in the face   ___

a) accept punishment
b) appear serious
c) be courageous
d) change the situation
e) grimace
f) obvious, evident
g) obvious, evident
h) defy, pay no attention to

The Price of Perfection

Getting the Point

The newspaper article on pages 27–28 describes the physical and monetary sacrifices some young people make in order to find the perfect face and body.

Skim the text by reading the titles and the first and last paragraphs of the article. Then answer the following question.

The author thinks that plastic surgery

a) is a good way to find success and happiness.

b) is never a good idea.

c) may help some teenagers, but not everybody.

d) should only be used for medical reasons.

Read the whole text to confirm your answer. Did you get it right?

Now that you've got the author's point of view, find the answers to Getting the Details.

Getting the Details

Circle the letter that corresponds to what you read in "The Price of Perfection". Find the lines in the article that support your choice and note the line numbers.

1 Karen had plastic surgery because
   a) she wanted to have perfect teeth.
   b) she didn't like her nose.
   c) her parents paid for it.
   d) she wanted to be slim.

   Line(s)

2 Plastic surgery for teenagers
   a) has become more popular.
   b) has increased by 15 percent since 1990.
   c) was not possible until recently.
   d) has decreased in popularity.

   Line(s)

3 Modern plastic surgery
   a) uses the same techniques as in 1950.
   b) offers much more choice than in the past.
   c) has become more expensive than it was 20 years ago.
   d) is only for girls.

   Line(s)

4 When Bruce had his nose reshaped,
   a) his parents paid for his surgery.
   b) the cost was covered by medicare.
   c) he got a job to pay for his surgery.
   d) he had to drop out of school.

   Line(s)

5 Carla Rice thinks that
   a) a beautiful body is important for happiness.
   b) there is too much pressure on teenagers to conform.
   c) plastic surgery is the best answer to insecurity.
   d) none of the above

   Line(s)

26

A better body and straighter teeth.

The Price of *Perfection*

by Janice Turner

Toronto Star

But can it give you happiness?

TORONTO – In many ways, Karen was your typical teen. Her appearance meant a lot to her and there was a lot about her appearance she didn't like.

She hated her double chin and felt utterly miserable in shorts or a bathing suit.

But unlike most teens, Karen's desire to look better didn't end with diet and exercise.

Not quite 16, and accompanied by her reluctant mother, she took her less-than-model-perfect body to a plastic surgeon.

Over the next three years – and with the help of a loan from her parents – Karen spent more than $4,500 to have the fat permanently removed from her neck, then her thighs, hips and stomach.

"I was frustrated because I felt I had done all I could," to slim down, said Karen, who is now in her 20s. "I wasn't happy. I wasn't satisfied with the way I looked."

Perfect bod, perfect face, perfect teeth. More and more teenagers are dishing out the bucks to improve their looks.

For decades, young people have flocked to surgeons for less noticeable noses and to dentists for straighter smiles.

Today, the options are much greater. Breasts can be resized, up or down. Saddle-bags a worry, tummy too flabby? There's liposuction. Chin or cheeks too hollow? There are implants.

The world of cosmetic surgery is just a consultation away. But some procedures have been linked to medical problems and the procedures don't come cheap.

Body contouring, for example, can cost anywhere from $1,000 to $4,000 and beyond. A new porcelain veneer smile, $500 plus per tooth.

And yet it's not just rich kids who are turning to cosmetic procedures. Some young patients gladly work nights, weekends and summers to cover all or part of the cost, surgeons say.

Young people like Bruce. At 17 he had a $3,000 nose job. In September, he returned to have his nose reshaping refined and for $3,000 worth of implants for his cheeks and chin.

"I guess I'm my own worst critic," said Bruce, a high-school student who delivered fast food for nearly three years to pay his surgical bills.

But why surgery?

"I wanted to be more photogenic," he said. "I wanted to be as perfect as I could be . . . I guess I'm kind of stubborn, that's all."

75 Plastic surgery, said Toronto-area Dr. Michael Bederman, has gone mainstream. Since 1990 he's seen a surge in interest from teens, who now make up about 15 per cent of his practice.

★   ★   ★   ★   ★

80 "There's a tremendous desire on the part of these girls to look like models," said Dr. Earl Farber, another plastic surgeon in Toronto. "They want to look like somebody maybe they're not. They want that 85 image."

The look? Large full lips, rolled out lips — even if it takes more than one try to get them full enough; a "natural" nose, not the pinched little nose that used to be a 90 dead giveaway.

Braces? Sure, some teens still get them. But the real rage is cosmetic dentistry — porcelain and plastic, and bleaching.

A designer smile can cost anywhere from a few hundred dollars to several thousand 95 dollars.

★   ★   ★   ★   ★

But is society's emphasis on appearance putting too much pressure on teens to both perform and conform?

Carla Rice, a consultant with the Woman 100 and Body Image Program at Women's College Hospital in Toronto, thinks so.

The teen years, she said, are often a time of profound insecurity, when youngsters are "struggling" to define themselves and 105 where they fit in the world.

"There's a myth in our society that if only you can look good, you'll feel good as well," said Rice, "that if you're physically beautiful and have a particular body size 110 or shape things will be good for you, you'll get what you want, you'll have success and happiness."

Many, no doubt, do end up feeling better about themselves, she said. Others may 115 find that, just like losing weight or getting a new hairstyle, plastic surgery is not a magic bullet.

Games People Play

Montaigne, the French philosopher, suggested that children's games are serious business. Today it seems that all games are not just serious business but big business. A look at sporting clothes and equipment is enough to convince anybody of this. Whether the games are played indoors or outdoors, whether they are intended to exercise the body or the mind, there is no doubting their popularity in everybody's culture.

Overview

Focus on Games

Before we examine the subject in more detail, let's start with a little survey of what you know and think about this topic.

Work with a partner or partners to decide what the word "games" means to you.

a) team sports

b) board games

c) card games

d) arcade games

e) computer games

f) all of the above

Now make a list of all the games you can think of. Classify them according to type.

A Bit of Background

Getting the Point

Skim the text on pages 31–32 by looking at the title and the first and last paragraphs. What is the main idea in the text?

a) Many games are not new.

b) Senet is an interesting game.

c) The origins of games are interesting.

d) Everybody likes games.

Now read the whole text to confirm your prediction. Did you get it right?

Now that you've got the main idea, find the answers to Getting the Details, pages 32–33.

A Bit of Background

The ancient Egyptians believed that life was simply a preparation for death, the state where everything that was pleasurable and enjoyable in life endured forever. Included in these pleasures was the ancient board game of Senet, and paintings of the afterlife often included depictions of players amusing themselves with this pastime.

What message do these pictures have for us today? Clearly, this is evidence from mankind's earliest historical records that games were counted among life's more pleasant aspects. And while today we might be hung up on Scrabble or Monopoly, it is interesting to know that the enormous popularity of games of this type is nothing new.

However, not all such pastimes began as innocent distractions.

Many board games in their original forms had a serious purpose, frequently associated with religious practices. Snakes and Ladders, for example, the children's race game, had just such a beginning in India. Originally, it was intended to play a more significant role in children's lives than mere amusement: it was designed to teach morality, with the ladders representing virtuous acts and the snakes, sins.

And those ever-popular playing cards were first employed in predicting the future. To this day there are still superstitions associated with certain of the cards making up a standard deck. The Jack of Hearts, the Queen of Spades and the jokers, to mention just a few, can be included in this category.

In the past, they were supposed to have mysterious and magical powers, and this element is often found in tales of the occult and supernatural in which the hero or heroine draws one of the cards, with disastrous consequences.

When we move to games like team sports, the stories about their lineage are even more fascinating. Take polo, the sport where players mounted on horses chase a ball with a mallet. It's alleged to have had its beginnings when victorious armies used the heads of their defeated opponents instead of balls, and swords and spears instead of mallets. The conquering army jubilantly raced over the field of battle celebrating its success by using the heads of vanquished adversaries for sport. It's a far cry from today's country-club atmosphere for polo players, isn't it?

Then there's the custom we are all familiar with—conquering teams being pa-

31

raded through the streets of their home base with the trophies they have won. This practice too had martial beginnings. It is the modern version of the Roman 80 "triumph"—a military parade held to display the loot captured in successful warfare.

Among Canada's contributions to games that have enjoyed worldwide endorse-85 ment are the board game Trivial Pursuit and the team sports basketball, hockey and lacrosse. This last item was invented by indigenous people, who called it "baggataway". It was the French settlers who 90 gave it the name lacrosse because they thought the stick used in play resembled a crosier, the stylized cross traditionally carried by bishops.

Slowly but surely this sport, which 95 appeals to both male and female competitors, is gaining acceptance around the world. It has already had its first international competition, with contenders from several countries including Japan, where it has gained phenomenal 100 popularity in the past few years.

When examined, most games have a fascinating history or origin. Whether they are played to enhance physical or mental prowess, to challenge fate as with games 105 of chance, or to provide pleasant social contacts, games are part of our human heritage offering multiple examples of our ingenuity and talent for amusement. The ancient Egyptians loved the game of 110 Senet enough to include it in the desirable things they wished to accompany them in the afterlife. We have other diversions today, some old and some new, but there's no denying that we are 115 just as fond of them as the ancients were of theirs.

Getting the Details

Circle the letter that corresponds to what you read in "A Bit of Background". Find the lines in the article that support your choice and note the line numbers.

1 The ancient Egyptians are mentioned in the first two paragraphs
  a) to explain the game of Senet.
  b) as a distraction.
  c) as a preparation for death.
  d) to introduce the history of games.

Line(s)

2 The board game Snakes and Ladders was originally designed
  a) to teach good behaviour.
  b) as an innocent pastime.
  c) in ancient Egypt.
  d) only for amusement.

Line(s)

3 Playing cards were originally used
  a) to play patience.
  b) to predict the future.
  c) to obtain magical powers.
  d) to teach morality.

Line(s)

4 Polo supposedly began
  a) as a way of fighting.
  b) with mallets and balls.
  c) at a country club.
  d) as a victory celebration.

Line(s)

32

5 The custom of parades for victorious teams originated

   a) in ancient Rome.

   b) in ancient Egypt.

   c) in France.

   d) in Canada.

Line(s)

6 The sport originally called "baggataway" was first named "lacrosse" by

   a) bishops.

   b) French immigrants.

   c) hockey players.

   d) native people.

Line(s)

7 In Japan,

   a) lacrosse has always been popular.

   b) there was an international lacrosse competition.

   c) men and women play on the same lacrosse teams.

   d) lacrosse has recently become very popular.

Line(s)

Vocabulary in Context

Identify each word in the first column as a noun, a verb, an adjective or an adverb, according to how it used in the text. Then match the word with the most suitable definition.

When you have finished there will be two unused definitions.

Words

1. depictions *(line 8)*   noun   m

2. diversions *(line 114)*

3. endured *(line 5)*

4. enhance *(line 104)*

5. fate *(line 105)*

6. jubilantly *(line 68)*

7. lineage *(line 55)*

8. loot *(line 81)*

9. pleasurable *(line 4)*

10. prowess *(line 105)*

11. vanquished *(line 70)*

12. virtuous *(line 36)*

Definitions

a) ability, skill

b) amusements

c) ancestry, history

d) conquered

e) decreased

f) destiny

g) enjoyable

h) increase, improve

i) joyfully

j) lasted, survived

k) moral, ethical

l) prizes

m) representations

n) vanished

Interview with Andrew Golding

Andrew Golding is a systems analyst who has a strong interest in games. In fact, he is a championship player.

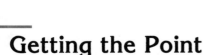

Getting the Point

Listen to the recording a first time to find the answer to this question.

Which game is Andrew particularly interested in?

_____

Getting the Details

Now that you've got the general idea, listen to the report again and try to find the answers to these questions.

1 The first board game Andrew learned to play was
   a) Monopoly.
   b) Scrabble.
   c) Snakes and Ladders.
   d) chess.

2 When Andrew was about six or seven, he found it
   a) easy to beat his parents.
   b) hard to beat his parents.
   c) hard to play five games in a row.
   d) easy to find long words.

34

3 Andrew went to his first tournament because
   a) his parents entered him for the competition.
   b) he went to a special school.
   c) he wanted to prove he was the best player in the world.
   d) he wanted to play five games in a row.

4 The day after his first tournament, Andrew
   a) played against a computer.
   b) went home early.
   c) thought he was the best player in the world.
   d) had a severe headache.

5 The advantage of playing on the Internet is that he
   a) sometimes plays against the computer at lunchtime.
   b) can play against people all over the world.
   c) is sitting across the table from his opponent.
   d) can go to the Montreal tournament.

6 Andrew likes his game more than other board games because it
   a) has an element of chance.
   b) is different from chess.
   c) is played all over the world.
   d) can be played on a computer.

Writing the Rules

Suppose that you want to explain a favourite game to a friend who has never heard of it.

In a composition of about 100 to 125 words, describe the main features of the game.

Before you write your composition, list the points you think you should cover. Arrange them in order so that your reader will have a good understanding of your game.

After you finish your composition, check your spelling and punctuation carefully.

_____

_____

_____

_____

_____

_____

_____

_____

_____

_____

_____

Verb Terminology

Why are verbs important?

They are the engines that power our thoughts and ideas. They give life to language. They describe our actions (what we *do*) and our states (what we *are*).

What do you need to know about verbs in order to master this important element of your language study?

- You have to be able to recognize and construct verb forms.
- You have to learn how to use verbs correctly.
- Also, you have to learn some terminology so that you can talk about verbs and use reference books.

Term	Definition	Examples
Main verb	The part of a verb structure that carries the meaning. It is always a single word.	She **reads** a lot. They are **going** to the game tonight. The Egyptians **played** Senet. I haven't **tried** that new game yet.
Auxiliary verb	A verb that combines with a main verb to form a compound verb. When a verb is used as an auxiliary it loses its own meaning.	**Does** she read a lot? They **are** going to the game tonight. What games **did** the Egyptians play? I **haven't** tried that new game yet.
Simple verb structure	A verb that is a single word.	They **read** a lot. We **are** students. She **has** two sisters. You **went** to bed early last night.
Compound verb structure	A verb that is composed of one or more auxiliary verbs and a main verb.	They **are going** to the game tonight. **Do** you **play** chess?
Base form	The primary verb element, from which all the forms of a main verb are derived. The base form is the same as the infinitive without *to*.	go play read try

36

Term	Definition	Examples
Present participle	The base form + *ing*. The present participle combines with the auxiliary verb *be* to form the continuous or progressive tenses.	going playing reading trying I **am inventing** a new game. I **was trying** to write the rules. I **will be selling** it one day.
Past participle	For regular verbs, the base form + *d* or *ed*.	played tried
	The past participles of irregular verbs are just that—irregular!	gone went
	The past participle combines with the auxiliary verb *have* to form the perfect tenses.	I **have invented** a new game. I **had studied** several possibilities first. I **will have finished** next week.
	It also combines with the auxiliary verb *be* to form the passive voice.	Hockey **is played** on ice. Senet **was developed** in Egypt. The game **will be televised**.

Double Letters

If the base form of a verb ends in a single vowel and then a single consonant, double the consonant before adding -*ing* or -*ed*.

grab + *ing* → grabbing

drop + *ed* → dropped

read + *ing* → reading

turn + *ed* → turned

But if the base form has more than one syllable, double the consonant only if the accent is on the last syllable.

for**get** + *ing* → forgetting

repro**gram** + *ing* → reprogrammed

ad**mit** + *ed* → admitted

de**vel**op + *ing* → developing

open + *ed* → opened

visit + *ed* → visited

Do you agree or disagree with these statements? Think of the arguments for and against.

In a class discussion, try to defend your ideas with force and conviction.

38

Luck

This is a report on a characteristic of games—not just games of chance—and of other aspects of life, too.

Getting the Point

Listen to the report a first time to identify the speaker's main point.

a) Persistent winners are fraudulent.

b) Luck cannot be completely explained.

c) If you are unlucky, skill counts for little.

d) Some people go through periods of winning streaks.

Getting the Details

Now that you've got the point, listen to the report again and try to find the answers to these questions.

1 According to the report, most people believe
   a) we can control luck.
   b) we can't control luck.
   c) luck plays a part in gambling and most games of chance.
   d) there's no such thing as luck.

2 Some people think talking about luck is
   a) coincidence.
   b) superstitious.
   c) a losing streak.
   d) a winning streak.

3 The premium-bond example showed
   a) you can only win a lottery-type game once.
   b) a few bond owners won repeatedly.
   c) there was fraud in the system.
   d) psychologists know why some people win more than once.

4 During their winning streaks, multiple winners
   a) were lucky at everything.
   b) won a lot of money.
   c) played tennis or team sports.
   d) were looking for answers.

5 By interviewing repeat winners, psychologists found
   a) empirical data.
   b) explanations.
   c) fraud.
   d) a mystery.

Auxiliary and Semi-auxiliary Verbs

There are three true auxiliary verbs in English: *do*, *be* and *have*. They combine with a main verb in the following ways.

Auxiliary Verb	Main Verb	Examples
Do (do, does, did)	Base form	She **does** not **work** here. **Do** you **like** this course? We **did** not **hear** the bell. **Did** he **go** with you?
Be (am, is, are, was, were)	Present participle	At the moment, we **are studying** verb forms. At that time, she **was living** in Sherbrooke
	Past participle	This product **is manufactured** in Quebec. They **were told** to wait here.
Have (have, has, had)	Past participle	They **have closed** the office early today. Suzanne **had studied** Spanish before she went to Mexico. She **has studied** Spanish for eight years.

Semi-auxiliary verbs are like true auxiliary verbs in one respect: they need a main verb to give them real meaning. Unlike true auxiliary verbs, however, they have specific meanings of their own, which we will study in a later lesson. They have only one form—they never add *s*, *ed* or *ing*.

Semi-auxiliary Verb	Main Verb	Examples
can, could, may, might, must, shall, should, will, would	Base form	She **can speak** Spanish. She **could speak** Spanish when she went to Mexico. I **must leave** now. I **will explain** everything later.

Applying the Rules

A. **Circle the verb form you need to complete the sentence, and cross out the other words in bold print.**

1. We could **used / using / use / to use** more practice time at the rink this year.
2. Did they **helping / help / helped** your playing strategy?
3. They might not **been / being / be** ready to join a league.
4. Can they **playing / to play / played / play** tennis?
5. Are they **eaten / eating / eat** after the game today?
6. Does he **knows / know / knowing** the rules of soccer?
7. You will **like / liking / liked / to like** this book of sports stories.
8. They didn't **promised / promise / promising** to get us tickets for the game.
9. We might **changing / changed / change** our hockey schedule this season.
10. We don't **wanting / want / to want** to play Scrabble.

B. **Provide the correct form of the main verb (the verbs in parentheses) to complete the sentences.**

1. They didn't _____ to play soccer. (want)
2. Do they always _____ to the arena? (walk)
3. Does she always _____ to the arena? (walk)
4. Can you _____ with them to the hockey game? (go)
5. Have you _____ your crossword puzzle? (finish)
6. He doesn't _____ how to play Yahtze. (understand)
7. She couldn't _____ how to play cribbage. (understand)
8. He has _____ a tournament schedule for us. (prepare)
9. We have often _____ about buying the new version of Clue. (talk)
10. We might _____ to get a different game instead. (decide)

C. **Underline all the main verbs in the text "A Bit of Background", pages 31–32. Circle the auxiliary and semi-auxiliary verbs. For each compound verb, identify the main verb as (a) a base form, (b) a present participle or (c) a past participle.**

And Then Along Came TV

Getting the Point

Read the first two paragraphs of the article to find the answer to this question.

This article is about

a) egg production.

b) a televised debate.

c) the influence of TV on sports.

d) the popularity of sports and game shows on TV.

Now read the whole text to confirm your prediction.

Did you get it right? Now that you've got the topic, find the answers to Getting the Details.

Getting the Details

Circle the letter that corresponds to what you read in the text "Then Along Came TV". Find the lines in the article that support your choice and note the line numbers.

1. The introductory paragraph gives you a clue by introducing you to a saying. What is the reason for this?
   a) To explain why game shows are popular.
   b) To show why television sports are popular.
   c) To show how beneficial television is.
   d) To describe the controversy about the influence of television.

   Line(s) ____

2. The concluding paragraph refers to the same saying. Why?
   a) To explain why television sports are popular.
   b) To show that there is no way to resolve the controversy successfully.
   c) To explain why certain events have a worldwide TV audience.
   d) To explain the popularity of game shows.

   Line(s) ____

3. The discussion of game shows in Islamic countries serves
   a) to illustrate how popular *Wheel of Fortune* and *The Price is Right* are.
   b) to explain features of the Islamic religion.
   c) to explain Islamic reactions to gambling.
   d) to prove how skilful humans are at adapting a winning formula to suit particular circumstances.

   Line(s) ____

4. The really big advantage of watching sports on television is that
   a) you can look around the playing field or arena.
   b) you can watch instant replays, often in slow motion.
   c) you see lots of advertising.
   d) you can watch historical footage.

   Line(s) ____

5. Some people say that the influence of television sports is beneficial because
   a) it keeps people away from gambling.
   b) it prevents people from becoming intellectual snobs.
   c) it encourages people to participate in different sports.
   d) it allows people to relax as couch potatoes.

   Line(s) ____

42

And Then Along Came TV

*I*t's like the eternal argument about the chicken and the egg—which came first? Many people are prepared to argue that the explosion in the popularity of team sports and game playing owes much to the influence of television. On the other hand, there are those who say that television has taken advantage of the appeal of these activities to attract viewers. No matter which side you're on, it seems unlikely that the debate will be resolved one way or the other any time soon.

What we can state for certain is that a lot of program hours on television are devoted to sporting events of all sorts. In fact, new networks devoted exclusively to sports have appeared. And while there are no TV game networks as yet, TV game shows indisputably have millions of loyal fans around the globe.

Numerous adaptations of popular game shows, most of which first appeared in the United States, can be found in almost every part of the world. *Jeopardy,* a quiz show depending on the knowledge players have of specific subjects, has many imitators. So do *Wheel of Fortune* and *The Price is Right.*

In countries where the Islamic religion predominates, game shows like the last two are frowned upon because they are considered a form of gambling, an activity not permitted in Moslem cultures. Undeterred, television producers in these countries create substitutes, toning down the element of chance and emphasizing the competitive knowledge-based component. This is yet another illustration that the appetite for game shows crosses cultures—if indeed such proof needs to be demonstrated.

It is also proof of how skilful humans are at adapting a winning formula to suit particular circumstances. But the question remains— would these

kinds of pastimes have any popularity at all if TV hadn't introduced them to new enthusiasts?

When it comes to sporting events on television, we once more find ourselves faced with the chicken-and-egg puzzle, and the same conflicting points of view.

There are the intellectual snobs who have nothing positive to say about televised sports, declaring instead that television is creating a generation of overweight couch potatoes who should be out there practising sports instead of sitting in front of the goggle box at all hours of the day and in every season of the year.

On the other hand, there are those who claim that the influence of television sports is beneficial. They maintain that TV has result-ed in much more participa-tion by people who were first introduced to sports through this medium. They cite the phenomenal growth in activities like tennis and golf to support their case.

Still others suggest that the appeal of sports on tele-vision may have something to do with instant replays. If you're at the arena or the playing field, you survey the crowd, chat with your companions, buy some-thing to eat and drink or listen to the commentary during lulls in play. If you're at home, you get advertising, true, but you also get a second chance to see interesting and critical points in the match, often in slow motion, which can add to the interest of the game. In addition, there are interviews with key players and discussions of strate-gies used in games past and present. Sometimes histori-cal footage of games and players adds spice to the television presentation.

Whatever the reason, there is no denying the appetite for sports on television. The summer and winter events of the Olympic Games grab viewers' attention around the globe thanks to satellite transmission. World Cup soccer matches do likewise.

Has the medium created this desire or does it need it to survive? That's like the chicken-and-egg debate. It's just another hotly contested argument, destined never to be concluded to anyone's satisfaction.

Sports Talk

Many idiomatic expressions are derived from sports and games. Try to decide which expression comes from which sport.

a) He's out in left field. (He suggested something ridiculous.)

b) I've got an ace up my sleeve. (I have a secret advantage.)

c) It's par for the course. (The result is what you would expect.)

d) She's backing the wrong horse. (She's supporting someone who cannot win.)

e) The ball's in your court. (It's your turn.)

f) They threw in the towel. (They abandoned something they were trying to do.)

_____ Baseball

_____ Boxing

_____ Card games

_____ Golf

_____ Horse racing

_____ Tennis

Affirmative and Negative Verbs

An *affirmative sentence* states something positive and a *negative sentence* expresses denial of a positive. In other words, affirmative corresponds to "yes" and negative to "no".

Negative Formation	Affirmative	Negative
If the main verb is a form of *be*, add *not* after it.	They **are** here.	They **are not** here.
If there is an auxiliary or semi-auxiliary verb, add *not* after the first auxiliary or semi-auxiliary.	The children **are** sleeping. She **has** finished. I **will** leave. They **will have** finished by 6 p.m.	The children **are not** sleeping. She **has not** finished. I **will not** leave. They **will not have** finished by 6 p.m.
If the main verb does not have an auxiliary or semi-auxiliary, add *do not*, *does not* or *did not* before the main verb and change the main verb to the base form.	They **know** us. He **knows** us. They **rented** a car. She **has** a little sister.	They **do not know** us. He **does not know** us. They **did not rent** a car. She **does not have** a little sister.*

* If the main verb is a form of *have*, you can follow this pattern or the one for *be* (She hasn't a little sister). Both are acceptable, though the *be* pattern is often considered to be British English.

Applying the Rules

Rewrite the following sentences to make them negative.

1. Many people are prepared to argue.

   _____

2. Television has taken advantage of sports to attract viewers.

   _____

3. It seems likely that the debate will be resolved. *(two possibilities)*

   _____

   _____

45

4. Producers tone down the element of chance.

5. TV is creating a generation of overweight couch potatoes.

6. They should be out there practising sports.

7. The influence of television sports is beneficial.

8. Replays can add to the interest of the game.

9. It's like the chicken-and-egg debate.

Which Side Are You On?

Like other businesses, professional sports sometimes have strikes and lockouts.

You represent one of the groups trying to negotiate an end to a dispute in a professional Scrabble league. The groups are:

- the team owners, who want to stop providing free coffee to the players
- the players, who want free sandwiches as well as free coffee
- the TV networks, who are losing advertising money because of the dispute
- the fans, who have nothing to do on Saturday nights because of the dispute

Before the discussion starts, think of the best outcome for the group you represent. Make a list of the arguments you can use.

Also make a list of the arguments you think the other groups will use. Prepare replies to these arguments.

During the negotiating session, defend your cause with force and conviction.

Morale Booster

Getting the Point

Skim the text on pages 48–49 by looking at the illustrations, the title and the headings.

According to this article, the game Networking
a) can motivate people.
b) is nothing more than a game.
c) is for introverts.
d) is fun to play.

Read the whole text to confirm your prediction. Did you get it right?
Now that you've got the main idea, find the answers to Getting the Details.

Getting the Details

Circle the letter that corresponds to what you read in "Morale Booster". Find the lines in the article that support your choice and note the line numbers.

1 Networking is
a) a card game.
b) a computer game.
c) a board game.
d) a team sport.

Line(s) _____

2 The game is sometimes used
a) by the Quebec government.
b) to test job applicants.
c) to criticize decisions.
d) to test employees' performance.

Line(s) _____

3 The inventor of the game
a) is a CEGEP student.
b) likes gardening.
c) is interested in psychology.
d) works as a biochemist.

Line(s) _____

4 The rules of the game are
a) short and simple.
b) complicated.
c) only on cassette.
d) printed on the box.

Line(s) _____

5 Which of the following statements about Networking is false?
a) Players must co-operate with each other.
b) When one player wins, the others lose.
c) Some of the cards are green.
d) The game involves acting imaginary scenes.

Line(s) _____

6 The volunteers who tested the game
a) enjoyed playing it.
b) had to admit their weaknesses.
c) had to think about their lives.
d) all of the above

Line(s) _____

Morale Booster

by BEE MACGUIRE

THE GAZETTE

MONTREAL – You know all about networking: the contact sport, natch. Homo sapiens have always gone in for it, ever since the first cordless phone – the prehistoric drum – was invented.

But have you heard about Networking, the board game? You will.

Networking, capital N, is a phenomenon of sorts. It's a controversial new Quebec-made form of entertainment. You play it with dice and rubber money, just like Monopoly, but this *jeu de société* has a biochemical side-effect. One enthusiast I spoke to put it like this: "It's the board-game equivalent of Prozac."

A single round of Networking, according to certain aficionados, is the equivalent of a week with Norman Vincent Peale, nose-to-nose, no extra charge for occasional belly laughs. The MacNeil-Lehrer News Hour has touted the game as a morale booster for veterans on the job-hunting circuit.

The Quebec government has been studying the game's motivational qualities with a view to using it to inspire its bureaucrats to dream bigger dreams. (The mind positively boggles at that one.)

One Quebec company I know of uses Networking as a psychological test for prospective employees. (A tell-tale combination of honesty, kidding around and acting out is required as you work your way around the board.)

Networking board game produces strange side-effect

Another firm hands each employee one of the game's attitude cards each week, complete with proverb and required on-the-spot performance. (For example, "It is easer to criticize other people's decisions than to stick to our own," followed by the instruction: "Stand up and repeat three times convincingly, 'I will stop criticizing critics' criticism.'")

Yikes. This is certainly a change from Parcheesi.

Non-chemical alternative

The news of this game comes at a propitious moment for Montrealers – smack in the middle of our midwinter slump. It might be a viable, non-chemical alternative to another proposed solution to our seasonally adjusted morale problem – adding Prozac to our municipal water supply.

But there's this little kinky detail. Does it work?

To test the biochemical effects of the game on humans, particularly on humans in a classically high-risk category, I contacted a firm called Murray Axmith Inc., career re-employment consultants, and asked if they could come up with a couple of volunteers – both in the middle of a stressful career transition – who would be willing to take a whack at it.

Last Friday, Tom Snabl and Sylvie Parayre convened at my house. They played networking. I did, too.

We learned the rules from an expert, Gérald Boivin, the game's inventor, who is not your garden-variety entrepreneur. He is an academic omnivore with a PhD in science and a degree in toxicology. He is a perennial student of psychology and philosophy, an accredited practicing CEGEP teacher and a computer whiz who helped launch Micro-Boutique.

A few years ago, Boivin divested himself of one of his titles – a summa cum laude diploma in shyness. He was painfully bashful all his life, he told me, until the day when his son, Thierry, dragged him off,

screaming and kicking, to a motivational seminar in marketing where he discovered the power of positive thinking.

Effect on the psyche

The chronic introvert came out of that seminar a new man and proceeded to turn his inquisitive brain to the subject of neuro-linguistics – the effect of positive thinking on the psyche. He read everything. He and his son Thierry then founded a company called Créations Earthrise Inc., which produces and markets inventions specifically designed to pass along the gift that Boivin got – as divertingly as possible.

But back to the game. There we were at the table, nerved up, a gang of strangers. Boivin explained the rules. They are quite complex – but the game includes a 20-minute tape of instructions as well as the standard written variety.

In Networking, we learned, your gain isn't another player's loss. Players have to get along, to communicate, sometimes on psychological striptease levels. When you draw a green card, for example, you have to come out of the closet. To tell the other players what your life's dream is, maybe. Or act out a hilarious scene, say waking up in your underwear in the middle of a shopping centre.

The other players then vote on whether you've pulled off your coup. If you have, off you go to a strategic networking card.

That night, as we played, we let cats out of bags, psychologically speaking, exposed weaknesses and strengths, recognized them in others and roared with laughter.

We were forced to think about our lives, our fears, our goals and our dreams.

As Parayre said afterward, "What really struck me is that you go beyond the pleasure of just playing a game. It's thought-provoking. It makes you feel richer."

Food, Glorious Food!

No need to theorize about the subject of this unit—it's one we all have an interest in. You'll read about food facts and fancies; find the way to bypass the pharmacy by eating the right combination of fruits, herbs and vegetables; look at how to break into the ice-cream market; give advice to Andrea's troubled correspondents; and write the results of your own personal survey of your classmates. All this and grammar too!

Overview

Reading

Listening

Speaking

Writing

Grammar

Idioms

Focus on Food Myths

efore we begin, let's check out some popular beliefs about food to see where you stand. Do you agree or disagree with the following statements? Can you find any evidence for or against these beliefs?

Share your findings with your classmates.

"The most important meal of the day is breakfast."

"Eating chocolate will give you skin problems."

"Spicy food will ruin your stomach."

"Eating a lot of red meat makes people aggressive."

"If you eat large quantities of fish, you'll be very intelligent."

Facts about Food

Getting the Point

Quickly skim the article on pages 53–54 by reading only the first few words of each paragraph.

Which of the following statements best expresses the writer's point of view?

a) You should always be very careful about what you eat.
b) As long as you usually follow a balanced diet, you can eat what you like.
c) It's O.K. to eat anything you like any time you like—no restrictions!
d) Vegetarianism is the most healthy way of life.

Read the whole text to confirm your prediction. Did you get it right?

Now that you've got the writer's point of view, find the answers to Getting the Details, page 55.

Facts about Food

Should you feel guilty because you rush out of the house every morning chewing on a bit of toast or munching on an apple because you just didn't have time to sit down to a good breakfast that included the recommended food groups: fruit or vegetables, cereals, dairy products and protein from an acceptable source?

The answer to that is an unequivocal no. You can forget the shame and relax. Breakfast habits the world over are just that—habits, like all the rest of the meals we eat during the day.

If you have grown up with a hearty breakfast, your body is conditioned to taking on a load of fuel in the morning and expects it. If, on the other hand, you've had the equivalent of a continental breakfast all your life, the mere thought of consuming juice, cereal, eggs, meat, pancakes, toast and a hot drink to wash it all down may make you decidedly queasy.

It all depends on where you come from and what you're used to having for the first meal of the day. Continental breakfasts have already been mentioned and, as one would suppose, they are the preferred first meal of the day of many Europeans. Inhabitants of warmer climates usually confine themselves to fruit and some kind of cereal grain, leaving their heavier meals until the later, cooler hours of the day.

Another factor to consider is that age and the time at one's disposal also play a part in the ongoing breakfast debate. Students are notoriously short of the latter element and they seem to be the ones most inclined both to skip breakfast and to worry about doing so.

Breakfast routines are as diverse as the people who've evolved them, and the best advice is to eat according to your specific tastes and needs and not worry about so-called "rules".

If you still feel the need to harass yourself about food and what it may or may not do to and for you, there's always that arch villain, chocolate. It has a fascinating history and a devastating power of addiction.

"Eat your breakfast—it's the most important meal of the day!"

53

It was first introduced to Europe from Spain's New World as an aphrodisiac drink. Then some enterprising soul discovered that mixing the supposed aphrodisiac powder with sugar and butter made an irresistible confection. Chocolate lovers have been trying to resist it ever since.

Does chocolate cause skin problems? Chocoholics of the world can desist from anxiety. Since 1969 dermatologists have been studying the situation to see whether there is any correlation between the consumption of chocolate and skin eruptions. The results of their research? No connection whatsoever.

Despite the fact that there are those who will swear to you that the mere mention of the mouth-watering treats causes their skin to go red and itchy, take courage. Ignore them and indulge in chocolate with a clear conscience and an equally clear complexion. Problem skin is much more likely to be caused by a lack of zinc in the diet than by chocolate.

Still, if you don't want to cast this delectable treat in a criminal role, you can turn your attention to hotly spiced foods or red meat. And you can start with the much-maligned chilis and other "hot" spices.

But you may be in for a disappointment, because research on the effects of these products on the tender linings of our stomachs has also come up with a not-guilty verdict. Apparently, that much-used over-the-counter drug, aspirin, has a much more devastating effect on the stomach than highly seasoned food. However, because the foods in question produce a sensation of heat in the mouth, the rumour persists.

And so does the notion that eating such

And so does the notion that eating such food directly before going to bed is a sure recipe for nightmares. The culprit here is not spicy food but any food. Edibles, if taken in quantity before retiring, might make for an unpleasant dream sequence or two. It's logical really. You've withdrawn from activity for the night but you've left your digestive system with a major workload. The resulting conflict often leads to a restless night and disturbed dreams.

Still another food legend is that eating too much red meat leads to aggressive behaviour. Once again, on closer examination, this turns out to be a major misreading of the information available. Perhaps the idea comes from the animal kingdom, where carnivores tend to be predators while herbivores are preyed upon. However, there is nothing to suggest that this applies to humans, who are omnivores.

Nor, for that matter, is there any evidence that eating large quantities of fish leads to the development of superior intelligence. If this were in fact true, penguins—who consume nothing but fish—would be ruling the world along with seals, who share a similar diet.

So there it is. You can omit breakfast and survive, snack on chocolate and still have a radiant complexion, consume chili and hamburgers to your heart's content and eat fish when you want to and not as an obligation towards your cerebral development. That is, provided that in general you follow the rules of good nutrition and eat a balanced, healthy diet.

Getting the Details

Circle the letter that corresponds to what you read in "Facts about Food". Find the lines in the article that support your choice and note the line numbers.

1 The writer of this piece thinks that breakfast
- *a)* should be composed of juice, cereal, eggs, meat, pancakes, toast and a hot drink.
- *b)* is a matter of habit.
- *c)* should include the recommended food groups.
- *d)* is the most important meal of the day.

Line(s)

2 The writer thinks that skin problems
- *a)* are often caused by chocolate.
- *b)* are not very serious.
- *c)* may be caused by a shortage of zinc.
- *d)* all of the above

Line(s)

3 The writer thinks spicy food
- *a)* causes bad dreams.
- *b)* is less dangerous than aspirin.
- *c)* can damage your mouth.
- *d)* can damage your stomach.

Line(s)

4 The writer believes that eating red meat
- *a)* is not good for humans.
- *b)* makes people aggressive.
- *c)* is not harmful to humans.
- *d)* is better than eating too much fish.

Line(s)

5 The writer believes that eating large quantities of fish
- *a)* is good only for penguins and seals.
- *b)* can be part of a healthy diet.
- *c)* makes people more intelligent.
- *d)* none of the above

Line(s)

Vocabulary in Context

Identify each word in the first column as a noun, a verb, an adjective or an adverb, according to how it is used in the text. Then find the most suitable definition.

Words		Definitions
1. chocoholics *(line 63)*		*a)* bad dreams
2. culprit *(line 98)*		*b)* clear, unambiguous
3. delectable *(line 80)*		*c)* foodstuffs
4. edibles *(line 99)*		*d)* guilty party
5. mere *(lines 19, 71)*		*e)* heavily criticized
6. much-maligned *(line 83)*		*f)* ordinary, simple
7. nightmares *(line 98)*		*g)* slightly sick
8. queasy *(line 22)*		*h)* people addicted to chocolate
9. unequivocal *(line 9)*		*i)* very enjoyable

Menu Comparisons

Most people have different eating habits depending on the day of the week it happens to be. Do you have a leisurely brunch instead of breakfast on Sundays? Or maybe you have to skip lunch on Wednesdays because of a class?

Choose two days of the week on which you usually eat differently. List your typical menu for each of these two days, and try to analyse the nutritional value of the two menus.

Use your notes to write a composition comparing your two menus.

Try to make your composition about 150 words long.

Interview with Don Kozsukan

Don Kozsukan is a young man in his mid-twenties. He works as a chef at the Montreal casino.

Getting the Point

Listen to the recording a first time to find the answer to this question.

The interview is about

a) how Don decided to become a chef.

b) his training in the restaurant business.

c) his real-world experience.

d) all of the above

Getting the Details

Now that you've got the point, listen to the interview again and try to find the answers to these questions.

1 Don began his studies
a) five years ago.
b) in the mid-eighties.
c) when he was 15.
d) recently.

2 Don became a chef because
a) he didn't like hotel management.
b) Lasalle College taught only cooking.
c) it was the only course available.
d) his summer job was in a hotel.

57

3 Don transferred to the ITHQ because
- **a)** Lasalle College didn't offer any on-the-job training.
- **b)** it was the official school for restaurant training.
- **c)** he didn't want to work in hotel management.
- **d)** he didn't want to be a chef.

4 At the ITHQ, Don learned
- **a)** the basics.
- **b)** how to work fast.
- **c)** real business.
- **d)** not to be a perfectionist.

5 How many meals do they prepare at the casino every week?
- **a)** 200
- **b)** 2,000
- **c)** 20,000
- **d)** 200,000

6 What does Don say about the Montreal casino as a place to work?
- **a)** There are too many employees.
- **b)** It's hard to become known.
- **c)** It's a good place to work.
- **d)** all of the above

Question Formation

In Unit 2, we saw how to create negative sentences.
Now we can study the formation of interrogative sentences or questions.
An interrogative verb form is used in "yes/no" questions—questions that expect an answer beginning with yes or no.

Question Formation	Affirmative	Interrogative
If the main verb is a form of *be*, put the verb before the subject.	They are here.	Are they here?
If there is an auxiliary or semi-auxiliary verb, put the first auxiliary or semi-auxiliary before the subject.	The children are sleeping. She has finished. I will leave. They will have finished by 6 p.m.	Are the children sleeping? Has she finished? Will you leave? Will they have finished by 6 p.m.?
If the main verb does not have an auxiliary or semi-auxiliary, add *do*, *does* or *did* before the subject and change the main verb to the base form.	They know us. He knows us. They rented a car. She has a little sister.	Do they know us? Does he know us? Did they rent a car? Does she have a little sister?*

** If the main verb is a form of *have*, you can follow this pattern or the one for *be* (Has she a little sister?). Both are acceptable, though the *be* pattern is often considered to be British English.*

Question Formation with Question Words

Another type of question, known as an "information" question, begins differently. The first word in an information question is normally one of the following eight question words: *what, when, where, which, who, whose, why, how.*

If the question word is the subject of the verb, the verb is in the affirmative pattern. Otherwise, the verb is in the interrogative pattern.

Question Words	Affirmative Pattern (Subject)	Interrogative Pattern (Object)
With *when, where, why* and *how* (used alone), only the interrogative pattern is possible.		*When are you leaving?* *Where do you live?* *Why are you studying geology?* *How did you get here?*
Who, what, which and *whose* can be the subject or object of the verb.	*Who is that?* *Who told you?* *What was lost?* *Which came first, the chicken or the egg?* *Whose are these?*	*Who did you meet after class?* *What does he know about it?* *Which do they prefer?* *Whose has she borrowed?*
What, which, whose and *how* can combine with other words to form question phrases. The question phrases can be the subject or the object of the verb.	*What animal left those tracks?* *Whose car is that?* *How many people are coming to the party?*	*What animal did they catch?* *Whose car did you borrow?* *How many people did you invite?*

Applying the Rules

Compose information questions for the following situations.

The word or words in bold print correspond to the question word—that is, they would be a short answer to the question.

Spaghetti is his favourite pasta.   Which _is his favourite pasta?_____

They cooked **spaghetti** last night.   What _did they cook last night?_____

1. They spend **a lot of** money on food.   How much _____?

2. People often eat out **to relax.**   Why _____?

3. The students had lunch **at noon.**   When _____?

4. The bakery is **on the corner.**   Where _____?

5. **The bakery** is on the corner.   What _____?

6. Most people like **Italian** food.   What kind of _____?

7. They should order **the lobster.**   What _____?

8. **Your** plate was on the table.   Whose _____?

9. They can buy vegetables **at the market.**   Where _____?

10. **The chef** recommends the raspberry mousse.   Who _____?

11. The chef recommends **the raspberry mousse.**   What _____?

12. **Fran** is studying at the ITHQ.   Who _____?

13. Fran is studying **at the ITHQ.**   Where _____?

14. Eric tried **four** different recipes.   How many _____?

15. **Eric** tried four different recipes.   Who _____?

60

Ask Andrea

Andrea's advice column is a well-liked feature in the local newspaper. Lately, she's been counselling people with food problems.

Work with a partner or in a group and decide which of Andrea's five possible answers is the most suitable. If you have a better suggestion, share it with the rest of the class.

Andrea, I'm Spanish and my fiancé is Irish. The trouble is that he wants me to cook potatoes with everything. He wants potatoes with his *tapas* and with his *paella*. I just can't seem to make him understand that this isn't right. I love him dearly but I'm not sure I can face a life of potatoes. What should I do?

Martyred Marta

Andrea's Answers

1. Order a pizza.
2. Eat TV dinners.
3. Let him do the cooking.
4. Cook the potatoes and don't argue with him. You can't do better than an Irishman. P.S. I'm Irish too.
5. Give him a print of Van Gogh's *The Potato Eaters*. He'll get the message.

6. _____

Dear Andrea,

I'm visibly pregnant and whenever I order coffee or wine in a restaurant I get a lecture from the serving person. How should I handle this?

Perplexed Mommy to Be

1. Forget it. You won't be "visibly pregnant" forever.
2. Tell those people that when you want their advice you'll ask for it.
3. Leave.
4. Burst into tears. Then they'll be sorry.
5. Shame on you, endangering your unborn child!

6. _____

Andrea, I need help.

Every time I take my girlfriend to a restaurant she embarrasses me by insisting on having gravy on her salad instead of dressing. What can I do about her bizarre taste?

Worried William

1. Stay away from restaurants.
2. Stay away from her.
3. Tell her she's making you uncomfortable and let her deal with it.
4. Don't let her order salad.
5. Carry a bottle of salad dressing with you and pour it on everything she eats.

6. _____

61

Dear Andrea,

My cousin, who's Chinese, like me, is marrying an Italian in June. Her parents have decided that all the Chinese families at the wedding banquet will have Chinese food and all the Italians will eat Italian. But not all the Chinese want it this way nor do the Italians. It's turning into such a big deal that my cousin is losing weight and her fiancé is losing his hair. What can they do?

Concerned Cousin

1. Tell your cousin she should talk her parents into considering a buffet dinner, with the guests free to choose East or West.
2. Your cousin should elope.
3. Obviously, your cousin doesn't know the golden rule— whoever has the gold makes the rules. If your cousin's parents are paying they'll do it their way.
4. Tell your cousin to consult a fortune cookie.
5. It could be worse. Your cousin could have Marta's problem.

6. _____

Food for Healing

Getting the Point

Look at the illustrations in the text on pages 63–64.

What type of food do you think the text recommends?

a) red meat

b) fruit and vegetables

c) vitamin supplements

d) chicken

Scan the text quickly to find specific examples of this type of food. How many can you find?

Now that you know what the text is about, read it carefully to find the answers to Getting the Details, page 65.

Food for Healing

Lately, doctors and laymen alike have developed a renewed interest in the curative powers of plants, fruits and vegetables. Of course, there has always been an abundance of information in folklore about the medicinal properties of various herbs. In fact, it is true to say that even now, at the end of the 20th century, much of the world's population uses herbs as primary medicine. What's even more amazing is that the active ingredients of more than 25 percent of modern prescription drugs are synthetic ver-

sions of herbal elements.

However, this does not mean that all of the claims made for herbal remedies should be accepted as the last word on the subject. Many of the assertions remain to be proven, since it is only recent-

ly that this branch of human knowledge has come in for serious study and evaluation.

And it isn't only herbs that are being analysed. These days it seems everyone is examining everything that passes our lips and assigning a value to it in terms of whether or not it contributes to good health and disease prevention.

Because preventive medicine is one way of cutting health-care costs, as well as contributing to the welfare of the population at large, interest in nutrition as an important element in a dynamic lifestyle is being encouraged. What exactly is known about the subject? Can we look forward to a future when doctors will be prescribing broccoli and carrots to cure our ailments rather than writing prescriptions for chemical cocktails? Instead of being told to pay a visit to the pharmacy, will we be invited to go to a fruit-and-vegetable stand in a farmer's market?

Chances are that's exactly what will happen, and here's why.

Food as medicine should be taken seriously:

63

research has found many links between health and certain foods, and the old saying, "An apple a day keeps the doctor away," seems to be true after all. Not only is the apple an excellent source of fibre, helping to lower cholesterol and aid in the prevention of cancers of the digestive system, but it also contains significant amounts of boron. Boron is one of those minerals our bodies need and it is important because it strengthens bones and helps to keep us alert. And that in turn suggests that

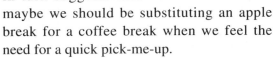

maybe we should be substituting an apple break for a coffee break when we feel the need for a quick pick-me-up.

But it isn't just apple eaters who can look forward to a longer, healthier life. Onions and garlic seem to have the same effect, while still other foods provide different types of benefits. Cranberries are good at fighting bladder infections, yogurt boosts the immune system and the family of vegetables known as crucifers—broccoli, cabbage and cauliflower—seem to contain elements that inhibit the development of cancer.

And, yes, chicken soup does have some kind of restorative power; it's thought to come from the bones used to make the soup stock. But beware of the skin on the chicken itself. It contains most of the fat—and that's one dietary factor that requires control.

The reason? Fat can be an enemy to good health if not consumed in moderation. Low-fat diets are recommended, but no-fat diets are not. Our bodies need a certain amount to function properly. That's a given. Fat provides energy. Paradoxically, too much can cause fatigue. So finding the happy fat balance is a must for good health.

To get back to the positive effects of fruits and vegetables, the benefits they provide are almost too numerous to catalogue.

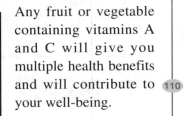

Any fruit or vegetable containing vitamins A and C will give you multiple health benefits and will contribute to your well-being.

Vitamin A is good for your eyes and your bones. It can also help reduce the risk of heart attacks and some cancers. Where can you find it? Yellow and orange fruits and vegetables like sweet potatoes, carrots, melon and apricots are good sources. So too are some greens such as spinach.

As for the C vitamin, it's almost an axiom that it is for cold prevention, but it is also necessary in forming the dentin of our teeth and the collagen in our connective tissue. Our chief dietary source of Vitamin C is citrus fruit. But—surprisingly—some green vegetables like broccoli and Brussels sprouts supply it too.

The next time you munch on a carrot stick or eat an apricot, take heart from the fact that you're doing yourself a good turn. Doing yourself a good turn by eating well is the principle to follow as we move into a new century. More information and more research on the healing power of food is sure to arrive, and it will almost certainly show us that what we eat not only sustains and adds to the enjoyment of life but may also prolong it if chosen knowledgeably and wisely.

Getting the Details

Circle the letter that corresponds to what you read in "Food for Health". Find the lines in the article that support your choice and note the line numbers.

1 Preventive medicine
   a) should be taught in school.
   b) is one way of cutting health-care costs.
   c) is the responsibility of doctors.
   d) has nothing to do with nutrition.

   Line(s) [____]

2 The medicinal properties of food should be taken seriously because
   a) we all have to eat.
   b) doctors are prescribing broccoli and carrots instead of pharmaceutical products.
   c) doctors like farmers' markets.
   d) none of the above

   Line(s) [____]

3 The old saying about an apple a day
   a) is silly.
   b) was created by the apple-growing industry.
   c) seems to be true after all.
   d) should be ignored.

   Line(s) [____]

4 People who eat onions and garlic can look forward to
   a) a longer, healthier life.
   b) losing their friends.
   c) using a lot of mouthwash.
   d) indigestion.

   Line(s) [____]

5 The vegetable family known as crucifers consists of
   a) broccoli.
   b) cabbage.
   c) cauliflower.
   d) all of the above

   Line(s) [____]

6 Chicken soup has some kind of restorative power because
   a) it contains vitamin A.
   b) it contains carrot sticks.
   c) it's made with yogurt.
   d) of the bones used in the soup stock.

   Line(s) [____]

7 Vitamin A
   a) will give you health benefits.
   b) will contribute to your well-being.
   c) can be found in carrots and apricots.
   d) all of the above

   Line(s) [____]

8 What we eat
   a) sustains life.
   b) enhances life.
   c) may prolong life.
   d) all of the above

   Line(s) [____]

Context without Vocabulary

In the following paragraph, some of the words have been replaced with nonsense words. Without referring back to the text, decide whether each nonsense word in bold print represents (a) a food or (b) a disease.

But it isn't just **bubbabu** eaters who can look forward to a longer, healthier life. **Ciccoca** and **doddadi** seem to have the same effect, while still other foods provide different types of benefits. **Faffufos** are good at fighting **gaggogo, huhhaho** boosts the immune system and the family of vegetables known as crucifers—**jujjijus, kikkokas** and **lillalas**—seem to contain elements that inhibit the development of **mimmumo.**

1. bubbabu ———
2. ciccoca ———
3. doddadi ———
4. faffufo ———
5. gaggogo ———
6. huhhaho ———
7. jujjiju ———
8. kikkoka ———
9. lillala ———
10. mimmumo ———

Growing Food in the City

A report from the Developing Countries Farm Radio Network

Getting the Point

Listen to the recording a first time to find the answer to this question.

Growing food in the city

a) is only possible in warm countries.

b) has several advantages.

c) can be expensive.

d) needs special equipment.

Getting the Details

Now that you've got the main idea, listen to the report again and try to find the answers to these questions.

1 Growing food in the city
   a) is not realistic.
   b) is sometimes called urban agriculture.
   c) is against the law.
   d) requires open fields.

2 A community garden can be started
   a) with neighbours.
   b) in a vacant lot.
   c) in an unused park.
   d) none of the above
   e) all of the above

3 Farming in the city
   a) can result in bruised and wilted food.
   b) can be expensive.
   c) can save you money.
   d) cannot be done because farming is possible only in the country.

4 Which of these statements is false?
   a) You can grow corn, melons or potatoes in parks.
   b) You can grow tomatoes in an old tire or plastic bag hung on a nail.
   c) You can't grow fruits and vegetables on rooftops.
   d) Getting started in urban agriculture means seeing the space around you with new eyes.

5 As a city farmer, you
   a) cannot grow potatoes.
   b) cannot save money.
   c) cannot grow as much per square metre as in the country.
   d) can grow more per square metre than in the country.

67

Present Continuous and Simple Present

Verb tenses are the forms of verbs that give information about the time of an action or state and about whether an action is complete or not.

Present Continuous Tense	Simple Present Tense
The *present continuous* represents an ongoing activity that is not yet complete or is temporary. Ongoing: You **are reading** this information about verb tenses. (You still have more to read). Temporary: They live in Napierville, but they **are spending** a few days in Drummondville.	The simple present tense communicates the idea of something permanent or generally true. It can also describe habits and abilities. Permanent: They **live** in Napierville. Generally true: The sun **rises** in the east and **sets** in the west. Habit: They **eat** pancakes every Sunday. Ability: We all **cook**.
The continuous form is restricted to verbs expressing actions or processes. Verbs expressing states are not normally used in the continuous form.	Some common verbs that express states are: *know, understand, mean, see, hear, like, love, hate, own, possess, resemble.* I **know** what you **mean**. They **own** a cottage in the Laurentians. She **resembles** her sister.
Use the present tense of *be* as the auxiliary verb, followed by the present participle of the main verb. I **am learning** You **are learning** He **is learning** She **is learning** We **are learning** They **are learning**	Use the base form of the verb for all persons except the third person singular. In the third person singular, add *s* to the base form. I learn You learn He learn**s** She learn**s** We learn They learn

Applying the Rules

Complete the following anecdotes with the appropriate tenses of the verbs in parentheses. Choose between the simple present and present continuous tenses.

A. If like me, you _____ (work) in a restaurant, you _____ (know) what stress _____ (be) and you _____ (understand) what I _____ (mean). If you _____ (not understand), I'll describe my typical day to put you in the picture.

I _____ (arrive) as usual at ten to prepare for the lunch crowd, and, as usual, the boss _____ (not bother) to say hello. Instead she _____ (give) me a distracted look and _____ (say), "You _____ (not wear) your uniform." She _____ (be) right! I _____ (not put) on my uniform until I _____ (start) work but she _____ (make) the same remark every day. Next she _____ (tell) me to check the menus and while I _____ (do) this she always _____ (interrupt) me to give me another job to do. By this time, I _____ (be) ready to quit!

B. My brother _____ (love) to cook but he always _____ (leave) the kitchen in a mess afterwards. He _____ (insist) he _____ (be) a culinary artist and so my mother _____ (have) no right to criticize. "I _____ (create) a masterpiece!", he _____ (declare). He _____ (use) the same excuse all the time when my mother _____ (object) to the kitchen chaos.

"No, you _____ (not be)," my mom _____ (answer); "you _____ (transform) my work space into an experimental laboratory."

"You _____ (laugh) at me," my brother _____ (reply). "Oh well, to be a genius _____ (mean) you must suffer and I _____ (suffer) now!"

Nutrition Survey

Interview your classmates about their food knowledge, experience and preferences.

You will be assigned one of the 30 topics listed below.

Before you start your interviews, prepare a series of questions on your topic so that you can obtain as much information as possible.

After you've completed the interviews, analyse the answers you have collected and report your findings to the class.

1. Experience of dieting
2. Cooking ability
3. Overeating
4. Favourite Quebec food
5. The four food groups
6. Favourite dessert
7. Birthday cake
8. Favourite fruit
9. Best food experience
10. Favourite pasta dish
11. Favourite kind of bread
12. Favourite junk food
13. Food you want to try
14. Food you would never eat
15. Vegetarianism

16. Breakfast (weekdays vs. weekends)
17. Favourite fish
18. Favourite ethnic food
19. Going to restaurants
20. Favourite Christmas food
21. Best national cuisine in the world
22. Favourite cheese
23. Favourite vegetable
24. Worst food experience
25. Favourite ice-cream flavour
26. Favourite food smell
27. Favourite drink
28. Favourite meat
29. Types of restaurants
30. Favourite snack food

Alberta Sisters are Entrepreneurial Winners

Because Sandra Rubin is writing about ice cream, she cleverly uses five food expressions to make her point more emphatically.

Sweet means both tasting like sugar, as ice cream does, and more generally agreeable.

Rocky road is the name of a popular ice-cream flavour and also means a difficult experience.

Took their licks means "had difficulties", but you also lick an ice-cream cone.

To scoop out is to dig with a round spoon, as in preparing an ice-cream cone.

Gobbling up is eating very quickly and greedily.

Getting the Point

Skim the article on pages 72–73 by reading only the titles and headings.

In which section of the newspaper was this article published?

a) the food section

b) the business section

c) the cultural section

d) the front page

Now read the whole text to confirm your prediction. Did you get it right?

Now that you've got the point of view, find the answers to Getting the Details, page 73.

71

Alberta sisters are entrepreneurial winners

Sandra Rubin

CANADIAN PRESS

TORONTO – The ice cream business has been sweet for Rhona and Robyn MacKay.

The sisters have made the family's tiny MacKay brand so popular that they've been designated the No. 2 asset of Cochrane, Alta., a town of 6,600 people.

Yesterday, they were recognized much further afield.

The MacKays received one of six 1994 Canadian Woman Entrepreneur of the Year Awards given by the University of Toronto. They were honored for their impact on the local economy.

Ice-cream pilgrimage

Stan Schwartzenberger, Cochrane's development officer, said the MacKays have made Cochrane a draw for many people in Calgary, who regularly make the 15-minute pilgrimage west for one of the famous cones. Cochrane considers its proximity to Calgary its No. 1 asset.

> **Fellow citizens say the ice-cream makers are their town's no. 2 asset**

"One of the most common sights we have on our streets is people licking ice cream," Schwartzenberger said in a telephone interview.

"When people hear Cochrane, one of their first responses is: 'Oh, that's the place with the ice cream.' That response speaks for itself."

It's estimated their ice-cream shop draws 10,000 to 15,000 people a week from outside the town during the peak season.

But it was a rocky road at first. Rhona and Robyn MacKay took their licks after buying their late father's general store and ice cream business in 1983.

In their 20s, they knew little about running a business and even less about making ice cream. And James MacKay died without leaving his basic recipe.

"We knew what it should look like and how it should taste but we didn't know exactly what was in it," said Rhona MacKay, 36, in Toronto with her sister to accept the award. "So we had to learn how to make what we wanted."

MacKay said she and Robyn, who is two years younger, also began having problems with long-time suppliers.

"The dairy started to let the cream slip, they had knocked the butterfat down and they were using inferior products as filler rather than straight cream," she said.

"The cream was changing and we didn't know why or what exactly was happening to it."

The sisters decided they needed technical know-how. So they went to the University of Guelph and then to Penn State University for a course on ice cream manufacturing.

"Then we came back to the dairy and said, 'OK, we've had enough. Let's do a little business.'"

In 11 years, the MacKays have done more than "a little business."

They've scooped out a lucrative niche with their 52 flavors of hand-mixed gourmet ice cream. In 1993, they registered $700,000 in sales.

"We've pretty well doubled everything from when we started running it – the number of employees, retail sales have doubled

and we've expanded in wholesaling."

Gobbling up market share

MacKay's Ice Cream is now sold throughout southern Alberta as well as parts of British Columbia and Saskatchewan.

The company has been gobbling up market share in an industry dominated by large national brands.

Their business plan calls for production to double every year, but only "as long as we can maintain control and our lifestyle," MacKay said.

"We don't want to sacrifice and grow so big that we're consumed with work 24 hours a day, 365 days a year."

Getting the Details

Find the lines in the article that mention the following points and note the line numbers.

1 Rhona and Robyn MacKay are very important for Cochrane, Alberta.

Line(s) _____

2 Being near Calgary is also important for Cochrane.

Line(s) _____

3 A large number of people visit Cochrane to buy ice cream.

Line(s) _____

4 Rhona and Robyn MacKay were young when they bought their father's general store.

Line(s) _____

5 They had a serious problem with a long-time supplier.

Line(s) _____

73

6 The sisters made a decision about something they needed.

Line(s)

7 Rhona and Robyn MacKay make money with their large number of flavours of ice cream.

Line(s)

8 They have significantly increased their business.

Line(s)

9 They sell their product in several provinces.

Line(s)

10 They have ambitious plans for the future.

Line(s)

Food Expressions

Complete the following statements with the most suitable expressions from the list on the right. There is one extra expression.

a) a good egg
b) bite off more than you can chew
c) chickenfeed
d) like two peas in a pod
e) the proof of the pudding
f) take it with a grain of salt

1. You can trust Madeleine. She's _____ . (a reliable person)

2. You shouldn't take seven courses next semester. Don't _____ . (try to do too much)

3. It doesn't matter what the machine looks like. Does it work? That's _____ . (the most important test)

4. Mark bought himself a new ten-speed bike. It cost $1700, but for him that's _____ . (an insignificant amount of money)

5. I never know which is Marie and which is Lucie. They're _____ . (identical)

Ecology Matters!

n this unit, you will read three texts about how environmental concerns shape our world and our lives. You will listen to two interviews about ecology and prepare an oral presentation of your own. You will also continue learning about verbs.

Overview

Reading

Listening

Speaking

Writing

Grammar

Idioms

Signs of Progress

The environment. Ecology. These are topics that seem to haunt us. Since the 1960s, when scientists and conservationists began sounding warnings about the future of the earth, has there been progress? Has what you have learned over the years about environmental problems caused you to change your lifestyle?

In a group, brainstorm with your classmates to make a list of examples of progress, large or small, in environmental matters.

When you have found 15 examples of environmental progress, examine your list and choose the three that will have the greatest long-term impact.

Explain to the class why you chose these three examples.

Wanted— A Modern-Day Noah

The passage on pages 77–78 is about endangered species—animals and plants in danger of extinction. You may be surprised to learn of the variety of species classified as endangered.

Getting the Point

Skim the text by reading the first and last paragraphs. Which of these statements best expresses the main idea of the article?

a) People should care only about the fate of wild animals and plants.

b) Trying to save domesticated species is a waste of time.

c) Efforts should be made to save all kinds of animals and plants.

d) Plants and animals that become extinct are no longer needed.

Read the full text to confirm your prediction. Did you get it right?

Now that you've got the main idea, find the answers to Getting the Details, page 79.

WANTED ...

A Modern-Day Noah

When we hear the term "endangered species", we usually think of giant pandas, Siberian tigers, cheetahs or large marine mammals. We rarely consider domestic animals to be endangered. Similarly, for plant life, the Brazilian rain forest or old-growth timber in the Pacific Northwest come to mind. We tend to think that only those species found in the wild are in danger of disappearing from the planet. The truth of the matter is that many varieties of plants and animals developed over the centuries to serve and nourish human beings are also threatened.

The Blonde Mangalitza, the only surviving breed of pig with a coat like a sheep's fleece, is still found in its native Hungary, but its numbers are dwindling. This rare domestic animal has found few to fight for its survival.

Fortunately, the same is not true of the giant donkey, the Baudet du Poitou. This creature, which also sports an unusual long-haired coat, was rescued from the brink of extinction and is now making a slow come-back in France, its homeland, and in America, where a small herd is being encouraged.

Some strains of poultry are also vanishing, being replaced by hybrids developed for increased egg production or higher ratios of meat to bone. One such victim is a British poultry variety, the Jubilee Indian game hen. Once widely raised for its dense and plentiful breast meat, this breed is now rarely seen on British farms except as a curiosity or a pet.

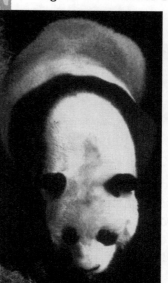

And it's not just animals that are in danger. Some older food plants have been replaced by new strains. Apples provide a good example. Many varieties are no longer produced by commercial growers because they were not suited to modern methods of shipping and storage.

These developments alarm some environmentalists, who argue that excessive hybridization and standardization can lead to weaknesses in plant stocks. The lack of diversity in the plant kingdom created by allowing older plant varieties to die out increases the danger of losing all members of a family to some new and unknown future parasite or plant disease. As an example of what can happen when there is a lack of diversity, they point to the great Irish potato famine of the nineteenth century, when the entire potato crop was wiped out. As the Irish had come to depend on potatoes, mass starvation resulted.

These conservationists also argue that the original plants have evolved over time and have become successful natural adaptations. Hybrids, in contrast, are artificial creations. Although they may be stronger in many ways than the stock from which they come, they may also be weaker in

some respects. We must therefore conserve the original plants.

To prevent the loss of traditional plant varieties, conservationists have established banks of "heritage" seeds. The seeds safeguarded in these banks will be used to strengthen current plant stocks if the popular hybridized varieties succumb to disease or parasites.

The concern for preservation of a species even extends to a deadly virus. In the 1980s, the World Health Organization reported that smallpox,

the disease, had been eliminated from our planet, but years later two research laboratories still held stocks of the virus in case of a recurrence of the disease or a mutant strain of a similar disease.

A decision was made to destroy these stocks, but the destruction was postponed several times. Some argued that if a new disease were to occur,

the smallpox virus might be valuable as a component in a vaccination against it. Those who wanted all samples of the virus eradicated said the disease was gone forever, and retaining even one sample was dangerous. By the time you read this, the issue may have been settled—or it may not.

Almost no one would argue against the need to maintain rare and exotic domestic animals or encourage banks of heritage seeds, but few are prepared to fight to prevent the extinction of a deadly virus—no matter how sound the scientists' arguments for keeping the virus.

Ecology matters! It matters very much. And finding reasonable solutions to our many unresolved ecological problems is a task that will be with us for years to come.

Getting the Details

Do the following statements (a) agree with the text, (b) disagree with the text or (c) not correspond to any information in it. If you answer (a) or (b), identify the lines that support your choice.

1 The Blonde Mangalitza pig is unique.

Line(s) _____

2 The Baudet du Poitou's country of origin is the United States.

Line(s) _____

3 Some hybrid breeds of poultry were developed for increased egg production and better ratios of meat to bone.

Line(s) _____

4 Many people died as a result of the Irish potato famine.

Line(s) _____

5 Hybrid plants are always stronger than the original plant stocks.

Line(s) _____

6 There was no disagreement about destroying the smallpox virus.

Line(s) _____

Understanding the development of the text

Answer the following questions by providing the relevant line numbers.

1 Which sentence in the first paragraph specifies the kind of animals that will be discussed later in the article?

Line(s) _____

2 Which sentence in the first paragraph summarizes the whole article?

Line(s) _____

3 Which paragraphs provide examples of the first subject (animals)?

Line(s) _____

4 Which sentence signals the transition from animals to plants?

Line(s) _____

5 Which paragraph explains why hybridization and standardization of plants can be a problem?

Line(s) _____

6 Which paragraph discusses a solution to this problem?

Line(s) _____

7 Which sentence signals the transition to the third subject?

Line(s) _____

8 Which paragraph presents the arguments on both sides of the smallpox issue?

Line(s) _____

9 Which paragraph rounds off all three subjects and prepares for the conclusion?

Line(s) _____

79

Interview with Dr. Lee Boyd

Dr. Lee Boyd is an associate professor of biology at Washburn University in the United States. She took part in an attempt to reintroduce an extinct species to its natural habitat.

Przewalski's horse, a small buff-coloured horse with a black mane, is the only species of horse alive today that is genetically distinct from the domestic horse. These wild horses are named after Nicolai Przewalski, a Russian explorer who found them near the border between Mongolia and China.

By the 1970s, Przewalski's horse was extinct in the wild.

However, zoos around the world had descendants of 12 horses that were captured around 1900. Recently two stallions, nine mares and a few foals were taken from zoos to Mongolia to be reintroduced to their original habitat.

Dr. Boyd in Mongolia

A Przewalski's horse in a zoo

One of the herds in the wild

Getting the Point

Listen to the recording a first time to find out whether the project was successful.

		Yes	No
1.	Did the horses adapt well to being out on their own?	◯	◯
2.	Did they know how to react to predators?	◯	◯

Getting the Details

Now that you've got the general idea, listen to the interview again. Try to find the answers to these questions.

1 Before Przewalski's horses were reintroduced into the wild, they were kept in large enclosures
   a) in Ukraine.
   b) in the Netherlands.
   c) for two years.
   d) for a hundred years.

2 When the gates were opened, one herd went out of its enclosure quickly
   a) because a foal was sick and had to be treated.
   b) to avoid predators.
   c) because the riders turned them back.
   d) because they were agitated after contact with humans.

3 The scientists decided that
   a) predators must be controlled.
   b) it was wrong to control predators.
   c) it was impossible to control predators.
   d) wolves are predators.

4 The Mongolian rangers' job is to
   a) check up on the horses.
   b) protect the horses from wolves.
   c) keep the horses out of the park.
   d) treat any infections.

5 When they were confronted with a wolf pack, the horses
   a) turned around and left.
   b) depended on the ranger for help.
   c) protected their foals from the wolves.
   d) didn't seem to know how to behave.

Pest Control

Here's a chance for you to argue the other side of the coin—why the populations of some species should at least be controlled and perhaps reduced.

Working in a group, prepare a brief presentation on controlled weeding out of excessive populations.

You may choose one of the following suggestions or find another example of your own. You will have to do some research outside of class.

1. Canada geese were introduced into Europe as an exotic ornamental species. In some areas they have now become pests. To protect native bird species, their numbers must be reduced.

2. Raccoons cause various problems in the city. They should be rounded up and shipped to northern areas where they can fight for survival like any other animal.

3. Seal populations must be controlled to allow fish stocks to grow. Reviving the fishing industry is more important than saving a few seals.

81

Why Ecology Matters

I f you were a conservationist, which endangered species would you fight hardest to preserve? Why do you think this species is important to our planet?

Defend your choice in a composition of about 200 words.

Introduce your subject in the opening paragraph. In the following paragraph(s), present the reasons for your choice. In the last paragraph, summarize what you have said or give a brief conclusion.

_____

_____

_____

_____

_____

_____

_____

_____

_____

_____

_____

_____

_____

_____

_____

_____

_____

_____

_____

_____

_____

_____

_____

_____

_____

_____

_____

_____

Semi-auxiliary Verbs

As you have already learned, semi-auxiliary verbs combine with the base form of the main verb and do not vary in form.

They refer to the present or to the future and have specific meanings. The following table lists the most important meanings.

Semi-auxiliary Verb	Meaning	Examples
can	ability	She can sing well.
	possibility	The alarm can go off at any time.
	permission (informal request)	Can we use the phone?
could	ability in the past	She could run faster last year.
	remote possibility	I could be wrong.
	permission (informal request)	Could we use the phone?
may	possibility, expectation	We may leave early.
	permission (formal request)	May we leave now?
might	possibility, uncertainty	We might go to a movie tonight.
must	obligation, necessity	We must do our homework.
	deduction	She isn't here, so she must be at home.
should	advisability, suggestion	You should do your homework.
will*	future	The train will arrive at 10 o'clock.
	intention	I will do it when I have time.
	agreement	If you ask her nicely, she will lend you some money.
would	conditional	Would you buy a car if you had enough money?
	agreement (polite request)	Would you open the door for me?

*The contracted form of *will not* is *won't*.

Applying the Rules

A. In the exercise below, circle the semi-auxiliary verb that illustrates the meaning required to complete the sentence.

1. The city _____ distribute recycling boxes on this street next April.

   Future: *a)* should *b)* will *c)* can *d)* must

2. _____ we declare this building a smoke-free environment?

   Permission: *a)* Will *b)* May *c)* Would *d)* Should

3. Cottage owners _____ try to use phosphate-free soaps.

   Advisability: *a)* should *b)* would *c)* must *d)* can

4. They _____ close the park because of the danger of forest fires.

   Uncertainty: *a)* must *b)* might *c)* can *d)* would

5. You _____ use my recycling box for your cans.

   Possibility: *a)* should *b)* will *c)* must *d)* can

B. In the following sentences, identify how the semi-auxiliary verb is used by circling the appropriate meaning.

1. She *should* walk instead of using her car all the time.

   a) conditional *b)* advisability *c)* necessity *d)* future

2. You *shouldn't* smoke here.

   a) advisability *b)* necessity *c)* ability *d)* permission

3. They *must* conserve more energy.

   a) obligation *b)* uncertainty *c)* conditional *d)* future

4. He *would* compost his garbage if he had the right equipment.

   a) conditional *b)* ability *c)* uncertainty *d)* advisability

5. She *will* represent her class at the ecology exhibition.

   a) ability *b)* permission *c)* uncertainty *d)* future

C. Supply appropriate semi-auxiliary verbs to complete the sentences. Use the preceding word in bold print to guide your choice.

If we are **able** to put a man on the moon, we _____ save the Siberian

tiger. The future of this species is **uncertain**: it _____ not survive. It is

advisable to do something now, so we _____ not delay. The **future** of

this magnificent beast is in our hands. It _____ become extinct if we don't

act. We have an **obligation** to save this creature and we _____ do so.

You're Right! You're Wrong!

There are usually two distinct sides on any ecological issue. People choose a side based on what they feel is "right" or "wrong". Their choices are influenced by factors such as deep personal conviction and economic necessity, and they will often defend their positions long and hard.

Hold a group discussion on one of the following topics.

Listen carefully to your classmates. Then decide what you think is right or wrong in the context. Prepare to defend your point of view.

1. The choice is to save trees or save jobs. Anyone knows jobs are more important.
2. Automobile use in urban centres must be restricted.
3. Forest fires are a natural phenomenon that humans should not try to control.

Cataclysms Past and Future

A cataclysm is a major disaster. Earth has been devastated in the past, and there are predictions of future cataclysms. While it would be nice to think humans could prepare for the next one, we know neither what it will be, nor when it will hit.

Getting the Point

Skim the text by reading the first and last paragraphs and then answer this question.

Many of the ecological problems we had in the past and might have in the future are

a) predictable.

b) controllable.

c) out of our control.

d) related to environmental abuse by humans.

Now read the complete text to confirm your prediction and answer the questions in Getting the Details, page 87.

Cataclysms *Past and Future*

Global warming, the hole in the ozone layer, overpopulation, desertification—all of these subjects lead to a feeling of pessimism about the future of our planet. True, they represent serious problems, but humans do have some measure of control over them. Other situations are entirely beyond human control. When the comet Schumacher-Levy struck Jupiter in 1994, we became aware of another potential hazard—collision with an asteroid from outer space.

Such a collision may have already occurred. Many theorists believe that a meteor collided with the earth several millennia ago, radically altering the conditions of life and resulting in the disappearance of the dinosaurs, the great creatures who had dominated our planet up to that point.

Predictions of a similar close encounter with a celestial traveller are more than just the stuff of science fiction. The odds on such a cataclysm occurring are better than those for buying a winning lottery ticket.

The oceans also hold many past and current mysteries. One of the first to recognize this was Jules Verne, the nineteenth-century writer of science fiction. He chose the depths of the seas and the centre of the earth as the sites for some of his most thrilling plots.

He didn't know when he wrote that researchers would uncover evidence of major cataclysms in the world's oceans. Kun Wang, a University of Ottawa researcher, has reported that approximately 250 million years ago, long before the age of the dinosaurs, 96 percent of marine species simply died out. The big question is, Why? While there is much speculation about what happened, no satisfactory interpretation of the incident has yet emerged. One hypothesis is that an event occurred similar to the one that precipitated the disappearance of the dinosaurs. Another is that an oceanic volcanic eruption created the catastrophe. The latter may be more plausible because evidence of similar explosions was recently uncovered.

Oceanographers exploring the Juan de Fuca ridge, off the coast of British Columbia, found both lava and towers of chemical-rich hot salty water pouring out of vents in the ridge. These phenomena may indicate that volcano-like eruptions occur on the ocean floor.

But—and this is the scary part, making real life stranger than a Jules Verne story—scientists have found primitive bacteria living in these scalding environments. And they hope to study them to see if they can be adapted for human use.

This has led to a controversy similar to the one surrounding the smallpox virus. In one camp are those who feel we should not introduce unknown bacteria to our environ-
80 ment; in the other are those convinced we should not reject this potentially beneficial initiative solely out of fear of the unknown.

This planet has known and survived devastating cataclysms. The most that people can hope is that there will be some warn-
85 ing as to when the next one will occur. There will be no hope of controlling it.

Getting the Details

Circle the letter corresponding to what you read in "Cataclysms Past and Future" and indicate the lines in the text that support your choice.

1 The comet Schumacher-Levy
  a) struck the earth thousands of years ago.
  b) figured in a Jules Verne novel.
  c) struck Jupiter in 1994.
  d) is still in orbit.

  Line(s)

2 Many people believe the age of the dinosaurs ended because
  a) of a hole in the ozone layer.
  b) a meteor collided with the earth.
  c) of overpopulation.
  d) of desertification.

  Line(s)

3 A close encounter with a celestial traveller
  a) is something plot writers for a blockbuster Hollywood movie might dream up.
  b) happens as frequently as winning a lottery.
  c) is ridiculous.
  d) is a possibility.

  Line(s)

4 A researcher from the University of Ottawa discovered
  a) an oceanic volcanic eruption.
  b) 96 percent of marine species died 250 million years ago.
  c) the Juan de Fuca ridge.
  d) the smallpox vaccine.

  Line(s)

5 The discoveries along the Juan de Fuca ridge are scary because
  a) they confirm volcanic-like eruptions on the ocean floor.
  b) of the lava.
  c) of the chemical-rich hot salty water pouring out of the vents.
  d) of the primitive bacteria living in these boiling environments.

  Line(s)

Unintended Consequences

Environmental measures sometimes produce unexpected results. Listen to this report to find out more.

Getting the Point

Listen to the recording a first time to find the answer to this question.

The subject of this report is

a) the increase in the population of mountain lions.

b) different ways of dealing with forest fires.

c) protecting endangered species.

d) the negative effects of some environmental decisions.

Getting the Details

Did you get the point? Now listen to the report a second time to get the details and answer these questions.

1 In California, mountain lions are

a) a protected species.

b) causing problems.

c) attacking people and domestic animals.

d) none of the above

e) all of the above

2 Environmental groups want

a) to allow hunting of mountain lions.

b) to agree with their opponents.

c) to preserve the status quo.

d) to move the lions to remote locations.

3 When it comes to forest management, U.S. environmental groups

a) believe in interfering with natural processes.

b) oppose intervention in natural processes.

c) think logging should be allowed on public lands.

d) believe in flexibility.

4 In Canada, human intervention on publicly owned lands

a) is never allowed.

b) is allowed only if forest fires approach human settlements.

c) is allowed.

d) is restricted to logging.

5 The best environmental policy is

a) to be flexible.

b) to judge each case on its merits.

c) a continual review of environmental measures.

d) all of the above

e) none of the above

Unit 4: Ecology Matters!

Simple Past Tense

In Unit 3, you studied the simple present tense. Here you will examine the simple past tense. This verb form describes actions or situations in the past.

Formation	Examples
For regular verbs, use the base form + *d* or *ed*. Note: If the base form ends in a *t* sound or a *d* sound, this ending is pronounced as an additional syllable.	A meteor **collided** with the earth millennia ago. An oceanic volcanic eruption **created** the catastrophe.
Many common verbs have irregular past tenses (see the list on page 149).	The comet Schumacher-Levy **struck** Jupiter. Jules Verne **wrote** about the depths of the seas.
The interrogative and the negative are formed with the auxiliary verb *did* and the base form of the main verb.	Why **did** the dinosaurs **disappear?** Jules Verne **didn't know** what researchers would uncover.

Applying the Rules

A. Practise using irregular verbs by completing this list.

For help, refer to the list of irregular verbs on page 149.

Present	Past	Present	Past
1. begin	_____	8. _____	kept
2. _____	broke	9. leave	_____
3. draw	_____	10. sit	_____
4. _____	drank	11. _____	spoke
5. _____	fed	12. undo	_____
6. feel	_____	13. _____	won
7. get	_____	14. write	_____

89

B. Provide the appropriate past forms of the verbs in parentheses.

When the Mongolian ranger _____ (find) the herd, he _____ (see) that

there _____ (be) a small pack of wolves confronting the horses. The horses

instinctively _____ (know) how to react to predators. They _____

(form) a circle with the foals in the centre, and the stallion _____ (face) the

wolves. It _____ (work). The wolves _____ (watch) for a while and then

_____ (turn) around and _____ (leave).

Tense Situations

Writing

As a noun, "tense" refers to the time of a verb. As an adjective, for example in "a tense moment", it means strained or full of tension.

Compose a short paragraph (of five or more sentences) on one of the following topics.

Explain why the situation was tense, using the simple past tense in the affirmative and negative forms.

1. Describe why you were late for an important appointment.
   Suggestions: car accident, memory problems, sick grandmother, disappearance of a pet.

2. Describe to the police a crime you witnessed.
   Suggestions: minor theft, bank robbery.

3. Explain to a parent why your bank balance is zero and you need to borrow money.
   Suggestions: to replace lost sports equipment, a big date

_____

_____

_____

_____

_____

_____

_____

_____

Animal Allusions

Many expressions compare good and bad human qualities to animal qualities.

In the following sentences, try to guess which animal completes each expression.

When you have finished, there will be one animal left. Can you provide an idiom with this animal?

a bat   bees   a dog   an eel   foxes   a mouse

1. She was sitting in the library, as quiet as _____.

2. When he walked into the physics lab, the students were as busy as _____.

3. I don't trust her; she's as slippery as _____.

4. Well, I don't trust either of them. They're both as cunning as _____.

5. Without her glasses, she's as blind as a _____.

6. _____

A "Tree Hugger" Recycles Fur

Fashion comes and goes. Until three decades ago, everyone wanted a fur coat. Now, many people refuse to wear fur. What is to be done with the many old furs stored away because they are too valuable to throw out?

Read about two fashion designers who believe this durable commodity should be recycled, creatively.

Getting the Point

Skim the text by reading the first sentence of each paragraph. Then answer the following question.

This article is about

a) why environmentalists want fur products banned.

b) how to eliminate fur products from the market.

c) two young fur designers.

d) efforts to strengthen the market for fur products.

Now read the whole article to verify your prediction. When you are sure of your answer, look for the answers to Getting the Details, page 95.

A "Tree Hugger" Recycles Fur

by Ann Brocklehurst

International
Herald Tribune

The racks of old fur coats in the designer Mariouche Gagné's workshop have been rescued from the basements and attics where they have been confined for years. Although still reviled by many as ecologically incorrect relics from another era, the newly cleaned and treated coats are about to be rehabilitated and recycled.

Gagné will turn the beaver, astrakhan, Chinese mink, opossum, fox and other pelts into her line of prizewinning fur clothing and accessories. She mixes the furs with leather, suede and re-used wool to turn out jackets, vests, backpacks, mittens, hats and scarves. Her designs also feature caribou-antler buttons inlaid with birds, fish and bears and sculpted specially for Gagné by Inuits in the Canadian north.

The aim is to make the old furs not only fashionable again, but environmentally acceptable as well. "I'm what you might call a tree hugger," said Gagné, 23, who after finishing design studies in Milan returned to Montreal to set up Harricana North Pole Canada earlier this year. "I wanted to start a company that would not pollute more and would create jobs."

Young designers such as Gagné are something of a godsend for the Canadian and international fur industries, which have in recent years been hurt not only by the animal rights movement but by global recession, an oversupply of fur and warmer weather. But thanks to the efforts of new, young designers, fur designs have become more sporty, relaxed and lighter weight. Pelts are being dyed new colors, and the emphasis is on sheered fur with its velvetlike pile. Now as sales start to climb, the industry is vigorously promoting its new designers and portraying fur as an environmentally sound product.

For Gagné, winning second prize in the Fur Council of Canada's 1993 design contest has generated much potential business. She was invited to Denmark for a short apprenticeship at the Saga international fur design center and was selected as a finalist in Japan's Gifu international fashion contest this year.

Despite the value of the hand-carved antler buttons, many sculpted

93

by the Inuit artist Peter Morgan, Gagné's prices remain competitive. Bags and backpacks are priced at about 200 Canadian dollars; coats 1000 dollars and jackets and vests, 500 dollars.

When Angela Bucaro, another Fur Council of Canada prizewinner, displayed her lightweight reversible ponchos, jackets and vests at the North American Fur and Fashion Exhibition in Montreal in the spring, many furriers could not even identify the pelts. "I'm doing fur in a way which is a little younger and untraditional," said Bucaro, 34.

Bucaro, who has clothing sales of more than 1 million dollars in North America and Europe, had no trouble selling her fur pieces to her regular retailers.

Even though she does not have the ecological bent of Gagné, she has also had to give serious thought to the issue of working with fur. "I've had people very close to me say, 'Angela, don't do fur. Why are you doing that?'" Bucaro said. "But, no, I didn't have any qualms. We all eat chicken and fish. They may not be as pretty as a seal. We all wear leather. Where do you draw the line?"

Fur manufacturers know that a better image will help them strengthen the current fragile recovery in their traditional markets after years, sometimes decades, of falling sales.

The industry's allies in the fight are unlikely bedfellows — the aboriginal trappers who still make a living from the fur trade and some of the top names in high fashion. In a promotional video for the Fur Council of Canada, both sides speak out. The trappers defend their use of a "renewable resource," while Edward Menicheschi, associate publisher for Vogue Europe, declares: "We are pro-choice for women and pro-fur."

Getting the Details

Circle the letter that corresponds to what you read in the article. Find the lines that confirm your choice and jot the numbers down in the space provided.

1 Mariouche Gagné makes her designs from
   a) old fur coats.
   b) leather.
   c) wool.
   d) all of the above
   e) none of the above

   Line(s)

2 She uses hand-carved buttons made from
   a) fish bones.
   b) caribou antlers.
   c) bear claws.
   d) bird feathers.

   Line(s)

3 She is trying to make her fur products
   a) win prizes.
   b) environmentally acceptable.
   c) expensive and exclusive.
   d) in Milan.

   Line(s)

4 After winning a prize from the Fur Council of Canada, Mariouche Gagné
   a) visited Denmark.
   b) won first prize in Japan.
   c) increased her prices.
   d) all of the above

   Line(s)

5 Some of Angela Bucaro's friends
   a) think she should not wear leather.
   b) tell her not to work with fur.
   c) think she should become a vegetarian.
   d) want her to work with Mariouche Gagné.

   Line(s)

6 The fur industry's allies are
   a) native trappers.
   b) top names in high fashion.
   c) native trappers and top names in high fashion.
   d) Angela Bucaro and Edward Menicheschi.

   Line(s)

95

UNIT 5

Technology —Here to Stay

In this unit, you are going to read about the positive and negative influences of technology on everyday life. You will discuss some of your experiences with technology and listen to others talk about aircraft safety standards and the *Star Trek* series. You will also study the grammar of conditions.

Overview

Reading

Listening

Speaking

Writing

Grammar

Idioms

Love It or Hate It?

Technology enables people to do more and to do it with greater efficiency and speed. Think of the simple task of washing clothes. In your grandparents' generation, it took all day to do laundry for a family. Today, the job requires little time and almost no physical effort.

Make a list of twentieth-century inventions. Then arrange your choices chronologically, starting with the earliest invention. Select one very important early invention and one later invention. Why were they important? How did they influence the society into which they were introduced?

Explain and defend your choices in a class discussion.

The Technology Explosion

Your first reading, "The Technology Explosion", presents an overview of technological development.

Getting the Point

Skim the text by reading the first sentence of each paragraph and then answer this question.

This text is about

a) how early technologies developed in isolation.

b) how technological innovation was lost in the past.

c) the increasing rapidity of technological development.

d) the development of transportation and communication technologies.

Read the complete text to confirm your prediction. Were you right?

98

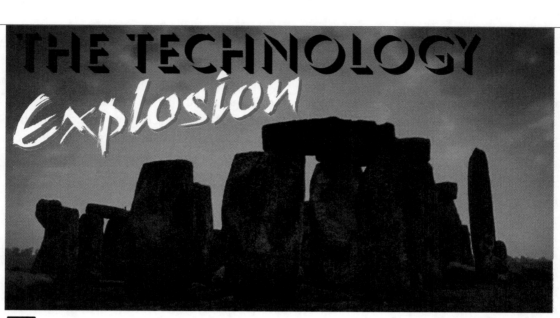

THE TECHNOLOGY Explosion

There has been a veritable explosion in the rate of technological development at the end of the twentieth century.

You can argue that there has been evolution in this area from time immemorial. And the proof is there for all to see, scattered throughout the world—Machu Picchu and Chichén Itzá in our hemisphere, the Great Wall of China in Asia, the pyramids of Egypt, the Greek temples and the Roman aqueducts in Europe—all of them vivid testaments to the technological ingenuity of civilizations of long ago.

Yet the great Mayan builders of Chichén Itzá knew nothing of the work of the pyramid-builders of Egypt. How could they? They worked on different continents and at different times. These societies had no awareness of one another and no means of communicating. Each developed in isolation.

Some of the wonders of the world—such as how the Egyptian pyramids were built—remain mysteries to this day. We can only speculate on how this task was accomplished, because no records exist to enlighten us.

One of the reasons for the incredibly rapid development of technology in our era is the fact that, since the industrial revolution began in the eighteenth century, techniques of innovation and experimentation have been diffused throughout the world. This has developed into a pattern for adapting and adopting technological developments, and building on them to produce further innovations, which makes it unlikely that our twentieth-century achievements will disappear in the same way as ancient technologies.

The progress of technological innovation was slow at first. Machines were invented to increase the production of goods, principally textiles. Gradually, mechanized manufacturing ceased to be an interesting novelty and became the norm for all kinds of production.

The next area to be touched by technology was transportation. Horse-drawn vehicles were replaced by machines—trains and trams, and then cars, airplanes and snowmobiles. (The horse left its mark, however, in the term "horsepower", originally used to express the number of horses it would take to provide the same force as a mechanical engine.)

Developments in communication were critical to the advancement of technology. The invention of wireless telegraphy and the telephone led the way, with radio and television following shortly after. And it is in the area of communications that technological evolution is now the most remarkable, indeed explosive.

Since the eighteenth century and the beginning of the industrial revolution, technology has developed through successive stages, from manufacturing processes through transportation and communications to the information age. With each stage, the pace of change has increased. Today, people are bombarded with a continuous stream of new products and services made possible by technology.

That is why the development of technology has been likened to an explosion. After all, isn't that what an explosion is—something that starts small but develops rapidly and can very quickly get out of control!

Getting the Details

Circle the letter of the phrase that best conveys the idea expressed in the text. Note the numbers of the lines that support your answers.

1 Historical monuments such as the pyramids in Egypt, the Great Wall of China and the Mayan temples of Chichén Itzá
- **a)** tell us nothing about the people who built them.
- **b)** were technically inferior.
- **c)** were early examples of knowledge shared among different societies.
- **d)** are vivid testaments to the technological ingenuity of civilizations of long ago.

Line(s)

2 Modern technologies will probably not be lost because
- **a)** everybody likes them.
- **b)** everybody can read.
- **c)** they are necessary for the survival of the human race.
- **d)** experimental techniques are widespread.

Line(s)

3 With the industrial revolution, people started
- **a)** building upon previously acquired knowledge.
- **b)** using machines to replace horses.
- **c)** believing machines would take over the world.
- **d)** working in factories.

Line(s)

4 The first machines invented during the industrial revolution were designed to
- **a)** improve transportation.
- **b)** develop communication.
- **c)** increase the production of goods.
- **d)** introduce the information age.

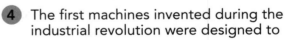

Line(s)

100

5 The power of machines is often described in terms of
   a) a mathematical formula.
   b) the cost to operate them.
   c) their function.
   d) the number of horses it would take to provide the same force.

   Line(s)

6 The term "explosion" is used to describe modern technological development because
   a) this development has gone through successive stages.
   b) it's already out of control.
   c) it started slowly but is growing more and more rapidly.
   d) of the effects of industrialization.

   Line(s)

Understanding the development of the text

Provide answers to the following questions and note the numbers of the lines that support your answers.

1. What characteristic distinguishes ancient Egyptian and Mayan builders from modern technologists?

   Line(s)

2. What factor is suggested as an explanation for the rapid expansion of technology?

   Line(s)

3. What makes it unlikely modern technology will be lost?

   Line(s)

4. What were the three stages of development in the industrial revolution?

   Line(s)

5. What stage have we reached today?

   Line(s)

6. What characteristic of this stage explains the title, "The Technology Explosion?"

   Line(s)

Interview with Alan Lea

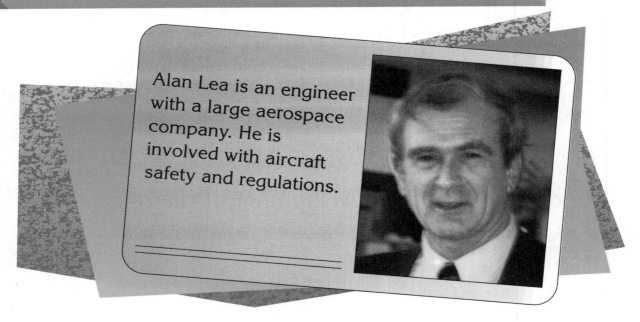

Alan Lea is an engineer with a large aerospace company. He is involved with aircraft safety and regulations.

Getting the Point

The first time you listen to Alan Lea discussing his work, keep this question in mind so that you can recognize the answer when you hear it.

Alan says:

a) New technology makes aircraft safer.

b) Manufacturers determine safety standards for aircraft.

c) Safety standards in the aerospace industry are dictated by governments.

d) Old technologies were more dependable.

Getting the Details

Now that you've got the general idea, listen to the interview again. Try to find the answers to these questions.

1 The accident near New Orleans was caused by

a) old technology.

b) weather conditions.

c) new technology.

d) a hole in the sky.

2 Alan Lea started his career as a

a) consultant.

b) government agent.

c) lawyer.

d) development engineer.

3 Alan says the real problem with airline safety is

a) too much government regulation.

b) not applying safety standards.

c) the human factor.

d) the equipment.

4 Alan thinks new technology

a) makes aircraft safer.

b) changes the circumstances.

c) is the same as the old technology.

d) is more dangerous than the old technology.

5 What benefit came from the accident near New Orleans?

a) The whole industry worked together to find and solve the problem.

b) The government forced the industry to co-operate.

c) The government created new regulations.

d) Twin-engined aircraft were taken out of service.

A Mind of Its Own

Sometimes a machine seems to have a mind of its own, usually when it doesn't work in quite the way it's supposed to. But as technology develops, machines are really becoming more intelligent in making decisions.

Choose a simple machine and predict what it will be like 20 years from now. In what way will it have a mind of its own?

Describe your machine to the class, using, if you like, an illustration of your concept.

103

Who's Answering the Telephone?

Imagine yourself in this situation. You dial a telephone number to obtain some information. A computerized voice answers and gives you a choice. It asks you to choose by pressing a number. The voice then gives you another choice, and so on. Eventually, you get the information you want, without ever speaking to anyone.

Write a short composition (approximately 200 words) describing this experience.

Start by explaining the situation. Then give a step-by-step description of what you did and what results you obtained. Use the past tense.

_____

_____

_____

_____

_____

_____

_____

_____

_____

_____

_____

_____

_____

_____

_____

_____

_____

_____

_____

_____

Conditional Sentences

Choices and decisions are often expressed in the form of conditions. For example, an automated information service might begin by saying, "*If* you want service in English, press 1."

If	*Then*	**Examples**
Conditional sentences express a choice between two possibilities.		If you want information on trains to Montreal, press 3.
Conditional sentences have two parts or clauses, often separated with a comma.		If you want to take the train, you must buy a ticket.
One part of the sentence begins with *if* and states the condition.	The other part is the *main clause*. It says what will happen if the condition becomes reality.	If you have a ticket, you can take the train.
Each clause has a complete verb.		If you **take** the train, you **will arrive** at 11:30.
The verb in the *if* clause is usually a simple tense. If the condition refers to the future, the verb is in the simple present tense.*	The verb in the main clause is usually a compound structure with *will* or another semi-auxiliary verb.	If you **don't take** the train, you **will have to get** the bus.
	The main clause may contain an imperative verb.	If you come by bus, **phone** me from the bus station.

* *Will* is not normally used after *if, when, as soon as, before, after,* etc., even when the sentence refers to the future.

Applying the Rules

Choose the appropriate verb form, recalling what you learned about verbs in the previous units.

1. If you need a more powerful computer, you **should upgrade / upgrade / upgraded / upgrading** your old one by adding more memory.

2. If she **wanted / wants / want / will want** to learn how to use this software, she must read the user's guide.

3. If he **finds / finding / find / will find** a good second-hand printer, he will be happy.

4. If she goes to the computer expo, she **see / sees / saw / will see** the latest software.

5. If he **go / goes / went / will go** to the computer expo, he will spend all his money.

6. If she takes a desktop-publishing course, we **give / gives / gave / will give** her a job.

Technobabble

Technology has always borrowed from the general language and has always created new words that have in turn been introduced into everyday use. Computers are no different.

Each of the words in bold print can have at least two different meanings. Try to identify the meanings from the list.

1. The electrical storm last night blew a **chip** in my computer.

   Meaning in this sentence: _____   Other meaning: _____

2. The knife wasn't sharp enough, so he **hacked** his steak into pieces.

   Meaning in this sentence: _____   Other meaning: _____

3. I'd really like your **input** before we decide which system to buy.

   Meaning in this sentence: _____   Other meaning: _____

4. The next version of the operating system will have a completely redesigned **interface**.

   Meaning in this sentence: _____   Other meaning: _____

5. The **mouse** was hiding behind her desk.

   Meaning in this sentence: _____   Other meaning: _____

General Meanings

a) a small rodent
b) a thin slice of potato, deep-fried
c) cut by hitting with a sharp object
d) opinions, suggestions
e) the area where two flat surfaces meet

Technical Meanings

f) a complex electrical circuit built on a small piece of silicon
g) a device for pointing at areas on a computer screen
h) data provided to a computer for processing
i) gained unauthorized access to a computer system
j) the way in which computer programs interact with humans

Real and Unreal Conditions

Not all conditional sentences express real possibilities.

	If	*Then*	Examples
R E A L	A *present real* condition expresses something that is really possible in the present or the future.		
	Use the simple present tense in the *if* clause.	In the main clause, use the simple present for a general statement.	If the temperature goes below zero, water freezes.
		For a future possibility, use *will* + base form of main verb (or another semi-auxiliary verb, depending on the specific meaning).	If the temperature goes below zero tonight, the water in the bird bath will freeze.
			If the temperature goes below zero, the water could freeze.
U N R E A L	A *present unreal* condition expresses something untrue or impossible in the present or the future.		
	Use the simple past tense in the *if* clause.	In the main clause, use *would* + base form of main verb.	If he found a summer job, he would be able to get a more powerful computer.
		Could or *might* can replace *would*, but the meaning of the sentence will change.	If he had a more powerful computer, he might be able to do his programming assignments on it.
	If the verb is *be, were* is usually considered more correct than *was* in the first and third persons singular.		If he were an experienced programmer, he could easily find a summer job.

Applying the Rules

A. Explain what the if clause means in the following present unreal conditions.

If he had enough money, he would buy a scanner.

He doesn't have enough money.

1. If she wanted a cellular phone, she would get one.

   _____

2. If I needed a new monitor, I would buy one.

   _____

3. If they were here, they would help.

   _____

4. If the teachers were here, we would ask them.

   _____

5. If we knew how to log on to the Internet, we would tell you.

   _____

B. Complete the following present real and unreal conditions by supplying an appropriate semi-auxiliary verb.

1. If the doctor had a cellular telephone, she _____ be able to respond immediately to emergency calls.

2. If he learns how to drive, he _____ be able to borrow his father's car.

3. If I get a degree in aerospace engineering, I _____ work for an aircraft manufacturer.

4. If I upgraded the hard drive, my computer _____ be faster.

5. If you didn't use your bank card so often, you _____ be able to save more.

6. If you were willing to try harder, you _____ get the hang of it.

C. Complete the following conditions by supplying appropriate forms of the verbs in parentheses. Add semi-auxiliary verbs if necessary.

1. If everyone adopted the new system, the results _____ (be) very significant.

2. If someone invented a new environmentally friendly mode of urban transport, everyone _____ (use) it.

3. If she _____ (have) access to the network, she can send the information to you via E-mail.

4. If we _____ (redesign) all our computer programs, we may have to change all our installations.

5. If you want to speak to a service representative, _____ (press) 2.

D. Practise using conditional structures by answering the following questions. Your answer must be a complete conditional sentence.

1. What will you do if you fail an important test?

   _____

2. What would you do if your hairdresser gave you a disastrous haircut?

   _____

3. What will you do if a stranger stops you on the street and asks you for money?

   _____

4. What would you do if your best friend asked to borrow a lot of money from you?

   _____

5. What will you do if your next-door neighbour plays loud music all night long?

   _____

6. What will you do if your friends have a surprise party for you on your birthday?

   _____

Time for Decision

bviously technology has given us great benefits. It has also created problems. On balance, has technology given us more disadvantages than advantages?

Take a position and be prepared to defend your point of view.

Benefits	Drawbacks	Where I Stand

Evaluating Technology in Our Lives

Getting the Point

Skim the text using an appropriate skimming strategy. Then answer the following question.

The author's main point is that

a) technological development makes people happy.

b) technological advancement has good and bad aspects.

c) machine power has replaced human power.

d) technological progress inevitably creates new problems.

Read the whole text to confirm your answer. Did you get it right?

Now that you've got the point, find the answers to Getting the Details, page 112.

110

Evaluating Technology in Our Lives

Consider the lives of people today. If they inhabit remote South Pacific islands, the upper reaches of the Amazon or the more isolated areas of sub-Saharan Africa, their lives are not much different from those of their ancestors. If they live in what is called a technologically developed society, however, their lives are radically different from those of their forebears. In these countries, machines now do much of the work formerly done by human beings: machine power has replaced human power and, in the case of agricultural communities, animal power as well.

You don't have to look too far for examples. Escalators and elevators climb for people, automatic vending machines pour drinks for them and remote-control devices change their television channels. Farmers now have automatic milking machines milking their cows, tractors ploughing their fields and a variety of machines collecting the harvest and rolling it up in neat bundles or sorting it and packaging it for market.

In several areas, notably transportation and communications, people's lives have been made easier and more interesting by these technological innovations. Air travel enables people

to cover vast distances in a short time, and telecommunications permit people anywhere in the world to communicate freely. The world, it can be argued, has become a global village.

Let's examine the meaning of this statement. What is the major characteristic of village life? In a village, everyone knows or knows about everyone else. Everyone shares the same concerns and the same interests.

111

And that is true to a certain extent of today's world. Thanks to satellite links, news and entertainment programming can be broadcast throughout the world—in other words, shared.

Technology has also introduced great improvements in health care and education. Although the benefits are unevenly distributed around the world, the positive results cannot be denied. For example, diseases and epidemics that once cut down whole populations are now effectively controlled through vaccination. Eradication of smallpox was the first such breakthrough. Then humans learned how to control diphtheria, tetanus, typhoid and polio, among other devastating diseases.

And the vast stores of knowledge accumulated during the whole of human history are now available to all who can read. Even more remarkable, the contents of the great art galleries of the world, multivolume encyclopedias and libraries of film are available in our own homes thanks to computers incorporating multimedia technology.

Despite the positive aspects of the rapid development of technology, there is concern about abuses. Stories abound of computer bulletin boards and networks being used to promote abusive propaganda and illegal activities, and there have been gruesome reports of people being murdered so their vital organs can be sold for transplant surgery. The widespread use of "feel-good" drugs such as Prozac makes Aldous Huxley's novel *Brave New World* seem like fact rather than science fiction.

Our lives are much easier than those of our forebears. We are healthier than they were, and we live longer. If they could compare their lives to ours, they would say we live in an earthly paradise beyond their wildest dreams of the future. Certainly we take for granted things they would consider miraculous.

But with all this technical progress, are people today happier than those who came before? Crime and violence have become modern-day plagues, seemingly always on the rise. The stress of urban living and hurried meals bring on heart attacks and other diseases our ancestors did not need to fear. As we rush through our busy lives, we are still searching for answers. Technology has given us a great deal, but not, perhaps, peace of mind.

Getting the Details

Complete the sentences below by circling the letters that correspond to what you read. Find the lines that confirm your choice and note the line numbers.

1 In the case of agricultural technology, machine power has replaced

a) farmers.
b) automatic milking machines.
c) tractors.
d) animal power.

Line(s)

2 Developments in transportation and communication have made people's lives

a) more stressful.
b) more boring.
c) more interesting.
d) more expensive.

Line(s)

3 "Everyone shares the same concerns and the same interests." *(lines 43–44)*

In the text, this sentence describes

a) technologically advanced societies.
b) village life.
c) the world we live in today.
d) satellite links.

Line(s)

4 The first disease to be controlled by vaccines was

a) tetanus.
b) smallpox.
c) diphtheria.
d) polio.

Line(s)

5 The populations of the technologically advanced societies are

a) happier than people were 200 years ago.
b) more violent than people were in ancient times.
c) more criminal than people were 200 years ago.
d) healthier and longer lived than people were in the past.

Line(s)

Vocabulary in Context

Identify each word in the first column as a noun, a verb, an adjective or an adverb, according to how it used in the text. Then match the word with the most suitable definition. When you have finished there will be two unused definitions.

Words		
1. abound *(line 78)*	_____	____
2. earthly *(line 94)*	_____	____
3. eradication *(line 60)*	_____	____
4. escalator *(line 18)*	_____	____
5. forebears *(lines 11, 90)*	_____	____
6. gruesome *(line 81)*	_____	____
7. plagues *(line 102)*	_____	____
8. ploughing *(line 24)*	_____	____
9. stores *(line 65)*	_____	____
10. unevenly *(line 54)*	_____	____

Definitions
a) ancestors
b) complete destruction
c) diseases that kill many people
d) exist in large numbers
e) horrible, disgusting
f) humanly, in a human way
g) keeps for future use
h) large quantities
i) moving staircase
j) not equally or regularly
k) of this planet, not spiritual
l) turning over the surface of the land

113

Living Longer, Living Better

It is widely held that people today live longer and better lives than those who lived around the start of the industrial revolution. Technology is credited for this vast transformation.

What is your opinion? From what you see around you and what you know of the lives of your forebears, do you expect to live longer and better? Has technology benefited you?

How might continued technological development affect you in the future?

Write a composition of about 200 words on this subject.

Don't forget to check your spelling and punctuation when you have finished.

"Beam Me Up, Scotty"

Getting the Point

Listen to the report a first time and answer this question.

According to this report,

a) science fiction can give us glimpses of future machines and lifestyles.

b) science fiction influences technological development.

c) the Russian space station *Mir* is modelled after the *Starship Enterprise*.

d) personal computers were invented by Mr. Spock.

Getting the Details

Now that you've got the point, listen again for the answers to these questions.

1. Trekkies are
   a) gadget lovers.
   b) space travellers.
   c) fans of a television program.
   d) computer hackers.

2. The communicator is similar to
   a) a PC.
   b) a cell phone.
   c) a stun gun.
   d) a laser beam.

3. Science fiction
   a) is not very popular.
   b) never predicts realistic innovations.
   c) sometimes predicts future developments.
   d) always makes accurate predictions.

4. *Mir*
   a) is a *Star Trek* character.
   b) is the fictional prototype of a space station.
   c) is the name of an American space shuttle.
   d) is the name of a Russian space station.

5. Dr. Valeri Polyakov is mentioned because
   a) he invented the stun gun.
   b) he was the first person to use a cell phone.
   c) he lived in space for more than a year.
   d) he was captain of the *Starship Enterprise*.

115

On-Board Computers Mean End of the Car as We Know It

Sometimes, science fiction accurately predicts the future. The following article relates how close to current reality American horror novelist Stephen King came when he wrote *Christine*, a story about a 1958 Plymouth.

Turn to the text on page 117. In it you will encounter the expression "R&D", which means research and development. The initials TRW stand for the name of a company. The term "fuzzy logic" refers to a type of computer program that does not follow the usual "if A then B" pattern but allows for complex interactions with the real world.

Getting the Point

Before you read the text, skim it by reading the headings and first two paragraphs after each heading.

Circle the correct answer to the following question.

According to this article, computerized cars will

a) soon have demonic powers.
b) sometimes take over from the driver.
c) drive themselves.
d) be too expensive for ordinary consumers.

Now find the answers to
Getting the Details, page 119.

116

Brian Bannon

On-board computers mean end of the car as we know it, Honda's chief engineer says

WINDSOR STAR

WINDSOR, Ont. — When Stephen King wrote his best-selling novel, Christine, about a '58 Plymouth with demonic powers, no one suspected how life would imitate art in the 1990s.

Computerized cars taking control from their drivers — although not with such bloody results as in Christine — was an underlying theme at the recent International Congress on Transportation Electronics in Dearborn, Mich., just outside of Detroit.

Several experts worried out loud about where computers are taking the automobile.

"It's the end of the car as we know it," Honda R&D's chief engineer Tsuneo Takahashi told the conference. Electronic control is moving beyond the engine, transmission and other functional things, he said. It is starting to take over human-like behavior, like vision, braking, steering and acceleration.

"Tickets are still going to drivers in accidents," Automotive News columnist Bill Diem said, "but there's been a shift in thinking. More and more, juries and the public hold cars responsible for keeping humans safe."

And owners want their cars to provide more than just stylish transportation, said TRW engineer Philippe Lemaitre. They want more comfort, convenience and entertainment.

The response of carmakers has been to add electronics and software control at the rate of about 13 per cent more each year, Lemaitre said. The public doesn't pay much attention because, unlike a new front grille, they don't see extra wiring and tiny computers.

Back in 1974, the only circuit boards in cars were in the radio and voltage regulator. Today there is more computer power in a new Chevrolet than was in the Apollo spacecraft that went to the moon.

The value of electronics on board the average car exceeds the value of the steel, and the wiring often reaches 15 kilometres in length.

I think I'll watch a movie at the drive-in tonight. Want to come along?

Practically every function is controlled by on-board electronics, and the next wave is for computers to tell drivers what to do and, in some cases, take over the driving.

It is already evident with anti-lock brakes and traction control which take over braking, with speed-sensitive steering and with air-bag systems which determine when an accident has happened and when to immobilize the driver.

WONDERFUL AND SCARY

Coming soon to your neighborhood are other wonderful, and slightly scary, ways computers will control your car.

Later this year, Canadians will be able to equip their vehicles with Delco radar systems that scan for nearby vehicles and objects and warn the driver of danger. The small radar boxes, adapted from the military, will be used on school buses first, to scan for children near a parked bus. They'll be available on transport trucks next year and on cars soon after that.

Delco Electronics president Gary Dickinson said the only reason Delco's collision-avoidance system doesn't automatically activate the brakes or steering to avoid danger is the company's fear of liability lawsuits if something goes wrong, and the avoidance manoeuvre actually causes an accident.

Most engineers believe that problem will be overcome, paving the way for cars that refuse to change lanes when another vehicle is approaching, and which slow or stop on their own when an obstacle is in their path.

A similar system called intelligent cruise control or active cruise control uses radar or lasers to track other vehicles ahead and adjust speed to maintain a certain distance. TRW says its system will probably be on a new car model by 1998 or 1999.

The first on-board navigation system is now available in the U.S. as a $2,000 option on the 1995 Oldsmobile 88 LSS. General Motors of Canada says it will be introduced in Canada later.

The system, made by Rockwell International, includes a display screen on the dashboard, a tracking system using satellites that continuously locates the car, and a database of city streets. Drivers just punch in an address, and the computer tells them by video maps and voice when and where to turn.

Other systems already available are automatic light and glare dimmers, remote keyless entry, car finders, monitors and controls for tire inflation, suspension, emissions, energy use, four-wheel drive, shock absorbers, theft prevention and interior climate, and all the parts for a complete on-the-road office.

Occupants can be monitored by a TRW system that changes the settings for seatbelts and air bags based on the weight and posture of whoever is sitting in the seat. Coming on stream in the next decade are on-line computers that give drivers updates on traffic, weather and other information.

The next step will probably be the expansion of so-called fuzzy logic in cars. Currently, some automatic transmissions and cruise controls use a form of fuzzy logic that decides what action to take based on probabilities and inputs.

Honda R&D engineer Shinichi Sakaguchi said it might be used in the future to predict and set steering, suspension and other systems that adapt to the individual driver, the road and weather. It will require much more computer power, he said.

There is a downside, of course. The days of doing even minor repairs on your engine, transmission or electrical system are gone. Control is locked in the car's central computer which requires another even bigger computer to diagnose.

Affordability is another issue. The growth of electronics during the past two decades has helped raise the price of new cars faster than incomes in North America.

Some in the industry say consumers are reaching the point where they aren't willing to pay for new safety and comfort features unless they see them as carrying high value.

"Consumers want it all, and at a very, very affordable price," Lemaitre said, but he said the demand for more electronics won't let up.

Getting the Details

Now that you've got the point, read the article again and try to find the answers to these questions.

1 Car manufacturers are computerizing cars because
   a) computerized cars will be safer.
   b) R&D engineers will lose their jobs.
   c) owners want more stylish cars.
   d) drivers will be superfluous.

   Line(s)

2 The value of the electronics in today's cars is
   a) the same as in 1974.
   b) 13 percent of the car's total value.
   c) more than the value of the steel in the car.
   d) equal to the cost of the electronics in the Apollo spacecraft.

   Line(s)

3 Delco car radar is based on systems first used
   a) in school buses.
   b) by intelligent cruise control.
   c) in transport trucks.
   d) by the military.

   Line(s)

4 The Delco car radar doesn't automatically control the brakes and steering because
   a) it is technically impossible.
   b) the company is concerned about possible legal action.
   c) it would be too dangerous.
   d) it can only track vehicles that are ahead, not behind.

   Line(s)

5 A satellite navigation system
   a) is already available in the U.S.
   b) is already available in Canada.
   c) will give drivers updates on weather and traffic.
   d) uses lasers to track other vehicles.

   Line(s)

6 The use of fuzzy logic
   a) will make it possible to repair the car's central computer.
   b) is part of the TRW system for controlling seat belts and air bags.
   c) will be increased but will need powerful computers.
   d) is not yet available for cars.

   Line(s)

7 There is a down side to increasing technology in cars because
   a) it makes them more expensive.
   b) it makes minor repairs difficult to carry out.
   c) all the computer technology on board requires a bigger computer to diagnose problems.
   d) all of the above
   e) none of the above

   Line(s)

You and the Job Market

n this final unit, you will consider the future—both your own and the future of the job market in a changing world. You will do writing assignments based on the readings, as well as oral activities and listening-comprehension exercises related to the theme. And, of course, you will also learn more about grammar—starting with ways of talking about the future.

Overview

Reading

Listening

Speaking

Writing

Grammar

Idioms

Looking for Experience

Before we move on to the future, check out your classmates' experience of the job market.

Find out who has worked at these jobs and what they learned from the experience.

Who Has Worked	Name	What They Learned
in a restaurant?		
as a salesperson?		
as a cashier?		
as a lifeguard?		
as a park monitor?		
in a garage?		
as a messenger?		
in an office?		
in a factory?		
as a musician?		
as anything else?		

Finding Your Place in the Job Market

Getting the Point

Skim the text by reading the title and the first three paragraphs. Then answer this question.

The purpose of this article is

a) to show you how to role play.

b) to give you information about interviews.

c) to provide you with a step-by-step approach to finding a job.

d) to summarize what you have learned at school about looking for work.

Read the whole article to confirm your prediction. Were you right?

Now that you know the article's purpose, answer the questions in Getting the Details, page124.

Finding Your Place in the Job Market

Sooner or later your school days end, and you find yourself on the job market looking for a permanent position. It happens to everyone, and yet very little in the education process provides practical preparation for this important step.

True, simulated job interviews and role playing are often done in class as exercises, but these activities barely scratch the surface and ignore some of the more important proceedings. Finding the right career is a serious business and it requires thoughtful approaches—because getting that first entry-level spot might be how you start yourself off on the fast track to success.

So sit yourself down with pencil and paper, or in front of your word processor, and take the first steps towards managing your career.

First of all, you should try to visualize your work, for now is the time to decide whether you really are suited to wearing a dress-for-success outfit five days a week and working in a large corporate structure, or whether your future will follow a different pattern.

Choose now whether you want to work in a group environment or not, for a large company or a small one, or for yourself. Consider every option and judge whether it coincides with your personality and life goals. The choice you finally make will have long-term effects on your life, and it's important to remember that.

Try also to imagine what your workplace will be like and what your daily routine will be. Check out the qualifications you will need for the work you see yourself doing, and compare them with those you already have acquired or are studying to obtain. This will give you a more realistic strategy for achieving your ultimate purpose.

That done, draw up a list of all the people—family, friends, employers past and present, neighbours, even teachers—who may be able to help you to that first important position. This is called networking. Essentially, it involves creating a bank of contacts for present and future reference. Your network will be revised constantly as you begin your working life, and you will at times be able to share it with friends and family, and also count on them to do the same for you. Don't be timid about approaching people. You'd be surprised at how helpful most human beings are. Sure, there will be an occasional rebuff, and you should be prepared to accept this. But on the whole you can look forward to a positive reception as you create your network.

Next, give a thought to how you want to proceed with the actual nuts and bolts of the job hunt. Are you going to prepare your own résumé or use the services of a specialist? The same question needs to be asked about the search itself. Do you want to do it on your own or put yourself in the hands of an agency? Before making decisions about these things, you should know what your priorities are (for example, what is more important to you: job opportunities or job security?). These services may cost money, and if you intend to take advantage of them, you should know exactly where you stand and be able

123

to convey this to anybody you pay to act on your behalf.

Finally, you will have to decide on tactics for job interviews.

Whether they are preliminary screening interviews or final hiring decision meetings, whether they are they are conducted by an individual or are team interviews, you should prepare yourself in advance.

In the matter of dress, you should be conservative and not flashy. You should ask questions and not just answer them. You should know something about the company or organization you are applying to.

You should try really hard to make a good impression without being too pushy.

After the interview, it might be a good idea to write a brief note to the interviewer thanking that person for seeing you. And don't hesitate to follow up with a telephone call a week or two afterwards if you haven't had any news one way or another. Sometimes the selection is a difficult one among several suitably qualified candidates, and it might just be the little things like a thank-you note or a telephone call that tip the balance in your favour. Often, it's just being in the right place at the right time that gets you the job—and making that telephone call just minutes after the interviewer has been told to hurry up and finish the hiring process is certainly in this category.

Finding your place on the job market is never an easy task. But with a combination of organization and determination the whole process can be converted from a stressful to a successful experience.

Getting the Details

Decide whether each of the following statements about the author's point of view is true or false. Find the lines in the article that support your choice and note the line numbers.

		Line(s)	True	False
1	The author is against practical preparation for job hunting during the education process.		◯	◯
2	The author is in favour of simulated job interviews and role-playing exercises.		◯	◯
3	The author recommends visualizing your future work.		◯	◯
4	The author is against networking.		◯	◯
5	The author is negative about having specialists prepare a résumé.		◯	◯

124

	Line(s)	True	False
6 The author recommends using employment agencies.	Line(s)	◯	◯
7 The author believes that agencies should establish your priorities for you.	Line(s)	◯	◯
8 The author suggests dressing in the latest fashions for an interview.	Line(s)	◯	◯
9 The author suggests writing a thank-you note after an interview.	Line(s)	◯	◯
10 The author says job searches are always stressful.	Line(s)	◯	◯

Vocabulary in Context

Identify each word or phrase in the first column as a noun, a verb, an adjective or an adverb, according to how it used in the text. Then match the word with the most suitable definition.

There are two extra definitions.

Words

1. corporate *(line 23)* _____ ___

2. entry-level *(line 12)* _____ ___

3. fast track *(line 13)* _____ ___

4. networking *(line 47)* _____ ___

5. nuts and bolts *(line 63)* _____ ___

6. rebuff *(line 58)* _____ ___

7. résumé *(line 65)* _____ ___

8. screening interviews *(line 82)* _____ ___

9. team interviews *(lines 84–85)* _____ ___

10. tip the balance *(line 105–106)* _____ ___

Definitions

a) of a large company

b) change the result

c) curriculum vitae

d) developing personal contacts

e) include

f) beginning, junior

g) interviews with several candidates at the same time

h) interviews to reduce the number of candidates to a short list

i) interviews with several interviewers at the same time

j) practical details

k) rapid promotion

l) rejection

125

Referring to the Future

There are several ways of referring to the future. Look at these examples from "Finding Your Place in the Job Market".

"The choice you finally make **will** have long-term effects on your life . . ." *(lines 31–33)*

"Are you **going to** prepare your own résumé or use the services of a specialist?" *(lines 64–65)*

Is there a difference between *will* and *going to?* For many situations, the answer is no. However, when you want to express a firm intention, the tendency is to use the present continuous of *go* plus an infinitive. For less precise statements about the future, *will* is generally preferred.

Form	Functions	Examples
The semi-auxiliary *will* + the base form of a main verb Note: The contracted form of *will* + *not* is *won't*.	General statements about the future	Sooner or later your school days will end.
	Promises	I will give you a lift to the bus stop. You don't have to walk. I won't forget to call you.
	Quick decisions	Okay, I'll go to the movies with you. I can leave this assignment till tomorrow.
Present continuous of *go* + infinitive	Definite intentions	When I finish my studies I am going to travel around the world.
Present continuous of main verb	Arrangements	I'm meeting her for an interview next week.

As a further example, look at these conversations.

Suzanne: Paul, are you free for lunch?

Paul: Yes, I am. Do you want to go to the new place on Saguenay Street?

Suzanne: Great! **I'll meet** you there in twenty minutes.

(Five minutes later)

Nicole: Suzanne, can you have lunch with me today?

Suzanne: Sorry, Nicole. **I'm having** lunch with Paul, but you can join us if you like. We're **going to try** the new place on Saguenay Street.

126

Applying the Rules

In each sentence, write the appropriate form of the verb in parentheses. In some cases more than one answer is possible.

1. Before you go to an interview, think about what you _____ (say).

2. You must also decide what you _____ (wear) to the interview.

3. She's written a new résumé and she _____ (send) it to about 20 companies.

4. I'm not sure what to do after I finish school. Maybe I _____ (continue) my studies or maybe I _____ (travel). I _____ (not look) for a job right away.

5. I know exactly what to do after I graduate. I _____ (look) for a job as a programmer.

6. If the economic situation doesn't improve, it _____ (be) very difficult to find a good job in my field.

7. They called him about an interview and he _____ (see) them next week.

8. "Did you get the job?"—"Yes, I _____ (start) on Monday."

9. We _____ (not forget) to send you the application forms.

10. Was that the doorbell? I _____ (see) who it is.

More Tense Situations

Imagine that you are in each of these situations. How will you react?

Write what you'll say and do in each situation, using appropriate future forms.

1. You followed all the advice about dressing for the interview but you find everybody who works here, including the boss, looks as though they have never heard of dressing for success. You feel uncomfortable and definitely overdressed.

   _____

   _____

   _____

   _____

2. A friend who works for the company told you how much people earn in the job you're applying for, but the interviewer offers you 20 percent less than that.

   _____

   _____

   _____

   _____

3. Everything about the job is too good to be true—the salary, the benefits, the working conditions, the opportunities for advancement. What's the catch? The company manufactures guns.

   _____

   _____

   _____

   _____

4. The interviewer offers you the job. You like everything about it, the working conditions, the benefits, the vacation and the work you'll be doing, but you don't like the salary. It's less than you hoped for. The interviewer explains that it is a new company with a hot new product and the outlook for the future is excellent.

   _____

   _____

   _____

   _____

128

Interview with Claire Rothman

Claire is a young woman in her thirties. She is a wife and mother and she works outside the home too. What Claire has to say will give you some idea of how to cope with career choices.

Getting the Point

The first time you hear the interview try to find the answer to this question.

Claire

a) chose her career early and stayed with her first choice.

b) thinks law is the best career choice for her.

c) has done many different things during her working life.

d) is a trend setter.

Getting the Details

Listen to the interview again to find the answers to these questions.

1 Claire decided to study law because
    a) she was passionate about it.
    b) there was a recession at the time and it seemed a good thing to do.
    c) her parents influenced her.
    d) she always dreamed of becoming a lawyer.

2 Which of these jobs did Claire *not* do after she gave up law?
    a) consulting   *c)* teaching
    b) editing   *d)* translating

3 Claire says the big disadvantage of her work is
    a) freedom.   *c)* flexibility.
    b) variety.   *d)* lack of security.

4 What is Claire's recommendation for students who might choose to follow in her footsteps?
    a) She strongly advises it.
    b) She has mixed feelings.
    c) She doesn't think anyone would want to follow in her footsteps.
    d) She advises against it.

5 Claire has heard that by the year 2010
    a) no one will have job security.
    b) all jobs will be temporary.
    c) three-quarters of all jobs will be temporary.
    d) no one will have benefits.

129

Visualizing Your Workplace

Do a survey among your classmates to see how all of you really feel about certain aspects of the job market.

Several questions are listed below: where you want to work, what kind of work you want to do, and the conditions you hope to find on the job.

Work in groups, with each group being responsible for surveying the class on several questions. When you ask the questions, don't just accept yes or no for answers. Go deeper and find out why. That will make your report even more interesting and informative!

Collect your information, and then analyse and present it.

Your group presentation should include a conclusion based on the information you collected. For example, if you find that nobody wants to work in a factory, or on a farm or at home, be sure to refer to this. Also mention the majority preferences.

When the reports are presented, take notes. Your next composition will be based on what you heard.

1. Place of Work	2. Type of Work	3. Working Conditions
• a big city, a small town or the country?	• with numbers?	• wear a uniform?
• your own country or another country?	• with criminals?	• loss of privacy?
• an office?	• making people look better?	• with all kinds of different people?
• a hospital?	• with sick people?	• with people like yourself?
• a factory?	• creativeness?	• working alone?
• a store?	• physical labour or activity?	• travel frequently?
• a theatre or a radio/television station?	• serving people in some way?	• be the boss?
• a farm?	• using persuasion?	• be part of a team?
• a hotel or restaurant?	• helping people psychologically?	• where you have to dress well all the time?
• a school, college or university?		• a job you can forget when you're not at work?
• home?		• shifts or weekends?

130

Preparation for Your Next Oral Assignment

Find a newspaper advertisement for a job you would like to apply for. Bring it with you to your next class. Your teacher will select a certain number of the jobs and set up simulated interviews. Some of you will have a chance to play the part of the interviewer, while others will fill the role of the job applicant.

Looking Ahead

Getting the Point

Skim the article using an appropriate strategy, and then answer this question.

This text shows

a) why job seekers should be pessimistic about the future.

b) why you can't trust economic trends.

c) how having a realistic attitude will benefit young job seekers.

d) that nothing is changing in the job market.

Read the whole passage thoroughly to check your prediction. Then answer the questions in Getting the Details, page 133.

Looking Ahead

What are the job prospects for young people today? Although most of them expect to have a great deal of difficulty finding and keeping a job, things might be a lot better than they think. For a start, some very hopeful economic trends are working in their favour. Let's have a look at them and analyse how they will benefit the young job-seekers of tomorrow.

DEMOGRAPHIC CHANGES

During the sixties, large numbers of jobs were created to accommodate the movement on to the job market of those born just after the Second World War, the baby-boom generation. The group following the boomers, sometimes called the baby-bust generation, is much smaller in number, with the result that as the boomers age and move out of employment to retirement more positions will become available for a much smaller number of potential employees.

The postwar baby-boom generation was very fortunate. There were plenty of jobs, and employers bent over backwards to please these people. They needed well-educated employees to take part in a continuing economic expansion. All this occurred when economic expansion was synonymous with job creation—before microchips ushered in the computerized phase of automation.

This is not the case today. A developing economy does not necessarily translate into job growth as it did when the boomers were beginning their careers. They were lucky. They were recruited from college campuses and could pick and choose among a multitude of great possibilities.

CHANGING ATTITUDES

That situation, unfortunately, was not the norm. Traditionally, finding that first opening has never been an easy task. The baby-busters are certainly witnesses to this, and it has modified attitudes to work considerably. This is a much more humble group than the boomers ever were. It consists of young people prepared to compromise, if necessary, to get that important first job and also to work hard once that goal is achieved. These young people are flexible, and their willingness to adapt themselves to the market has trained them well for the global competitiveness of the nineties.

Baby-busters could never be called spoiled brats, an accusation frequently levelled at the boomers.

They don't expect to have opportunities served up to them on a silver platter. They know they have to promote themselves and take chances. In short, they definitely don't have an attitude problem when it comes to work.

Another factor working in this generation's favour is that most of the members of this group have partly or totally financed their own education. While they were studying, they were also working—and the variety of part-time and temporary jobs many of them have held has given them a much more realistic appreciation of what's really going on out there in the real world.

132

80 Furthermore, during their lifetimes, they have seen the pace of technological change accelerate and have taken it in their stride.

85 Change is something they've grown up with, and it holds no terrors for them. They welcome it. They've gone from a Walkman to a CD player, from VCR cassettes to video-disc players and CD-ROMs without batting an eyelash. 90 Changes in the workplace will hold no terrors for them: change is their way of life. And the one thing we can all bank on in the future is change—rapid and dramatic change. The technology 95 explosion ensures it. The last half of the twentieth century began it, and the next century will see it carry on.

All those who can adapt to this situation will do well, so the baby-bust gen- 100 eration should find itself at home in this milieu. After all, change and adaptation is the story of their collective lives.

HOW BLACK *IS* THE PICTURE?

All things considered, the picture is not as black as some would like to paint it. 105 Certainly the familiar world of work the boomers know is not the one the baby-bust generation will find themselves in. That world—where one selects a career and stays with it for a lifetime—is fast 110 becoming a thing of the past. Young entrants to the job market know this and have strategies for dealing with it. They also know that the dream job they would do anything to get might 115 not be available right now, but prospects for its turning up in the future look better than they have for several years. They're patient. They're prepared to wait for the realization of their 120 goals. But above all they are realistic, which is their best guarantee of success.

Getting the Details

A. Circle the letter of the option which corresponds best to what you read.

1 According to this article,
  a) demographic changes are working in favour of the job seekers of tomorrow.
  b) demographic changes are working against the job seekers of tomorrow.
  c) the baby-boom generation will continue to saturate the job market.
  d) nothing will change in the job market of the future.

Line(s)

2 Young job seekers of tomorrow can expect
  a) difficulty in finding a job.
  b) some very hopeful economic trends.
  c) difficulty in keeping a job.
  d) the unemployment situation to get worse.

Line(s)

133

3 The generation following the baby-boomers

    a) is a much smaller group.

    b) is sometimes called the baby-bust generation.

    c) is much more humble than the boomers.

    d) none of the above

    e) all of the above

Line(s)

4 Baby-boomers were lucky because

    a) many of them were recruited into the job market directly from college campuses.

    b) there were plenty of jobs available.

    c) they could pick and choose among a multitude of good possibilities.

    d) none of the above

    e) all of the above

Line(s)

5 The world in which one selects a career for a lifetime is

    a) the world of the present.

    b) the world of the future.

    c) fast becoming a thing of the past.

    d) something we all regret.

Line(s)

6 For the baby-bust generation, change is

    a) something they've grown up with.

    b) something to fear.

    c) something they can't accept.

    d) something they find unfamiliar.

Line(s)

7 The baby-bust generation

    a) is flexible.

    b) knows it has to promote itself.

    c) knows it has to take chances.

    d) none of the above

    e) all of the above

Line(s)

8 The best guarantee of success for members of the baby-bust generation is that

    a) they are humble.

    b) they are spoiled brats.

    c) they expect jobs to be handed to them on a silver platter.

    d) they are realistic.

Line(s)

9 This text is principally about

    a) baby-boomers.

    b) positive future trends in the job market.

    c) technology and the job market.

    d) demographic changes.

Line(s)

B. Evaluate the following statements to see whether they agree with what you read.

	Line(s)	True	False
1 Mixing studies and work is not helpful.		◯	◯
2 The baby-bust generation is not adaptable.	Line(s)	◯	◯
3 The baby-bust generation is a bunch of spoiled brats.	Line(s)	◯	◯
4 Baby-boomers were often called spoiled brats.	Line(s)	◯	◯

134

Class Profile

For your writing assignment, you are going to give your reactions to the survey you and your classmates conducted on visualizing the workplace. From the answers to the survey questions, you should have a good idea of the kinds of work and conditions everyone would choose.

Use this information to write a class profile on working preferences.

In your composition, you will probably be able to use the simple present and simple past tenses. You may also need to use a form for the future. In any case, you can refer to the grammar sections of this and other units to help you make the right decisions. And don't forget the basic punctuation you saw in Unit 1. Tie all these things together to make this last writing assignment your best.

Past Continuous Tense

"While they were studying, they were also working . . ." (lines 73–75)

Like the present continuous, the past continuous tense describes a temporary or incomplete action.

Form	Function	Examples
Past tense of *be* + present participle of *main verb*	Describes a past action that continued for a limited time.	We **were living** in Paris five years ago.
	Distinguishes two past actions, one of which (past continuous) was interrupted by the other (simple past).	They **were watching** TV when the telephone **rang.** Jane **was trying** to make an omelette when she **dropped** the egg carton.

Applying the Rules

Answer these questions in complete sentences.

1. This year you're attending CEGEP. What were you doing last year?

   Last year, I _____

2. Most of us are preparing for the end of the session.
   What were we doing three months ago?

   Three months ago, most of us _____

3. Who were you talking to when I saw you in the cafeteria?

   When you saw me in the cafeteria, I _____

4. What were you thinking about when the teacher asked you a question?

   When the teacher asked me a question, I _____

5. What were you doing in the library when the fire alarm went off?

   When the fire alarm went off, I _____

6. What was he cooking when the power failure began?

   When the power failure began, he _____

7. Where were they going when we passed them in the car?

When we passed them in the car, they _____

8. What were they printing when the printer ran out of paper?

When the printer ran out of paper, they _____

Excuses, Excuses!

Since the past continuous can express an action that was interrupted, it is often used in making excuses when something has gone wrong. For example, "I'm sorry, Aunt Matilda. I was just dusting your Ming vase when it fell on the floor and broke", or "I'm sorry I'm late for class. I was waiting for the bus when I saw a hold-up take place and the police . . ."

Compose a creative excuse for each of these situations.

1. The car you borrowed from a friend has a cracked windshield.

_____

_____

_____

2. When you take out your résumé to give it to a potential employer, you see that it has a large coffee stain on it.

_____

_____

_____

3. On your second day in a new job, you crash the company's computer network by trying to install a game program.

_____

_____

_____

4. You are late for an important job interview.

_____

_____

_____

137

In Three Easy Payments

We all know that getting a job isn't easy these days. But cheer up. There are a lot of experts who are willing to share their know-how—for a price. But is their advice worth the money?

Getting the Point

Listen to the recording a first time to find the speaker's point of view.

In this report, the speaker is _____ the advertised book.

a) enthusiastic about

b) the author of

c) cynical about

d) serious about

Getting the Details

Listen again to discover the reporter's comments on these points.

1 What kind of food does the book say you should avoid at a lunchtime interview?

a) artichokes

b) boiled lobster

c) spaghetti

d) spinach salad

2 How much does the book cost?

a) $49.95

b) US$49.95

c) US$49.95 plus $6.00 shipping

d) $49.95 plus $6.00 shipping

3 What is supposed to irritate interviewers?

a) gold earrings

b) mini-skirts

c) men's gold bracelets

d) jewellery in general

4 Which of these was supposed to make women look like losers?

a) eating spinach salad

b) a certain type of blouse

c) gold bracelets

d) being overqualified

5 Which of these was mentioned as a question or a comment you might hear at an interview?

a) Name two weak points of your previous boss.

b) How could you have done better in your last job?

c) Why should I hire you?

d) Are you willing to travel?

Present Perfect Tense

Form	Function	Examples
Present tense of have + past participle of main verb	Describes experience or present relevance of actions that took place in the past.	She **has worked** in the tourism industry. (She has experience.) He **has applied** to almost fifty companies. (He should get some interviews.) I've **studied** German but I've never **had** a chance to practise it. (I can't speak German.)
	Describes an action beginning in the past and continuing into the present. The sentence often contains a time expression with *for* or *since*. *For* shows the length of time the action has continued. *Since* shows the starting point of the action.	I've **lived** in this neighbourhood all my life. He **has worked** very hard in all his courses. She **has studied** engineering **for three years**. He **has worked** for that company **since 1993**. She **has been** interested in entomology **since she was a little girl**.

Applying the Rules

Form the present perfect tense of the verbs in parentheses.

If necessary, consult the list of irregular verbs on page 149.

1. Our sales team _____ (meet) every goal since September.

2. Judy _____ (sell) more stock than anyone else for three months in a row.

3. They _____ (be) in my working group since the beginning of the month.

4. He _____ (not have) his salary increased for ages.

5. What _____ (you do) with my calculator? I lent it to you a week ago!

Living on a Shoestring

The words and expressions in bold print are associated with jobs and work.

Read the text and try to guess their meanings.

The average **working stiff** believes in the **work ethic** and simply tries to earn enough to avoid joining the **bread lines** outside food banks. Whether these people are employees or self-employed, running a **shoestring** operation such as a **mom-and-pop** corner store, their goal is just to earn enough to be **breadwinners** for their families. They are not **fat cats** in Cadillacs. They are not the **movers and shakers** of commerce. They are simply people trying to earn an honest living.

1. Working stiffs are
   a) people who suffer from arthritis.
   b) hardworking people.
   c) military veterans.

2. The work ethic is
   a) community service as an alternative to a prison sentence.
   b) an agreement between unions and management.
   c) a belief in the social and personal value of work.

3. Bread lines are
   a) poor people waiting for free food.
   b) extremely long loaves of French bread.
   c) the roped-off waiting areas in a bank.

4. A shoestring operation is
   a) a store that sells shoelaces.
   b) a business with very little money.
   c) involved in some kind of illegal activity.

5. A mom-and-pop business is
   a) any small family-owned business.
   b) a convenience store.
   c) a store that sells soft drinks.

6. A breadwinner is
   a) someone in a bread line.
   b) a person supporting a family.
   c) a specialized job in a bakery.

7. Fat cats
   a) are rich people.
   b) meow less than thin cats.
   c) sell illegal drugs.

8. Movers and shakers are
   a) alcoholics.
   b) influential people.
   c) a religious sect.

Present Perfect vs. Simple Past

Examine this dialogue.

Interviewer: **Have** you ever **used** accounting software?

Applicant: Yes, **I've used** XyCount on a PC and Ariel on a Mac.

Interviewer: Oh, **you've worked** on a Mac? Where **was** that?

Applicant: It **was** a course I **took** at the CEGEP.

We very often begin a conversation in the present perfect tense and change to the simple past tense when the conversation moves to specific details of actions that took place in the past, even if time is not mentioned.

Rule	Right	Wrong
If there is a specific reference to past time or past events, use the simple past tense.	Have you used the photocopier today? I have learned to type. She has worked part time since she was 16. He has studied math in CEGEP. (He is in CEGEP now.)	Have you used the photocopier yesterday? I have learned to type three years ago. She has worked part time when she was 16. He has studied math in high school. (He is in CEGEP now.)

Applying the Rules

Provide the appropriate form of the verbs in parentheses. Use only the simple past, past continuous and present perfect tenses.

If necessary, consult the list of irregular verbs on page 149.

1. I _____ (prepare) a list of questions to ask at my interview.

2. I _____ (prepare) my list last night.

3. While he _____ (work) for a telephone answering service two years ago, he _____ (have) a lot of amusing experiences.

4. While we _____ (wait) for the meeting to begin yesterday, we _____ (review) the month's sales figures.

141

5. Our sales team _____ (meet) every goal since the beginning of the season.

6. We _____ (go) to the management strategy course last night.

7. He _____ (not have) his salary increased for ages.

8. I _____ (prepare) this presentation especially for the brainstorming session.

9. Betty _____ (plan) to move to another department when our supervisor _____ (offer) her a promotion.

10. What _____ (you do) when

    I _____ (telephone) last night?

    I _____ (leave) an urgent message for you but

    you _____ (not return) my call.

11. Mary _____ (find) the job of her dreams.

12. No one _____ (hear) from Charles since he was transferred to Vancouver. And no one _____ (see) him since then.

Writing Your Résumé

Now try your hand at creating your own résumé. The model on the opposite page shows you how to proceed. It goes without saying that there are many ways to write a résumé and that your curriculum vitae will develop as your experience and training increase throughout your career. For the time being, however, provide as much information as you can within the structure you have before you. Use a black pen or a pencil and write over the pale coloured words.

142

Résumé of

Your Name

Your street address

City, province

Postal code

Telephone number(s)

Position Applied For

Career Goal

Education

Institution

Subject   date

Institution

Subject   date

Work Experience

Company

Job title   dates

What you did

Company

Job title   dates

What you did

OTHER

References

Name and address

Name and address

Name and address

date of résumé

143

Practising for the Job Interview

It's time to play the role of either an interviewer or applicant. Work on the job offer your teacher has given you.

- If you are to be the interviewer, think of a series of suitable questions to ask the job seeker.
- If you are the person to be interviewed, try to anticipate the kinds of questions you are going to be asked and have some answers ready. Also think of some questions you could ask about the job and the working conditions.

Work in groups before you do the interviews. Compare the job offers your teacher has given you and put your heads together to develop effective strategies for the interviews you are going to simulate.

Good luck to all participants!

Shifting Gears

This is the introduction to *Shifting Gears,* by Nuala Beck. In spite of its title, it's not a book of car talk.

Getting the Point

To find out what the subject of the book really is, skim the text quickly by reading only the beginning of each paragraph. Then answer this question.

Shifting Gears is about

a) doom and despair.
b) changes in the economy.
c) the old economy.
d) numbers and trends.

Read the whole text to confirm your answer.
Did you get it right?

Now find the answers to Getting the details, page 147.

Shifting Gears

Introduction

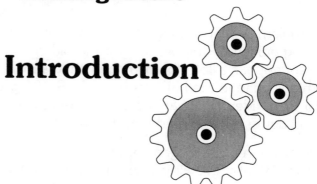

With the century drawing to a close, apocalyptic visions are again dancing in people's heads. You hear it on the street and read it in the news headlines and best-selling economic scare books: "The economy is doomed. This recession will never end. It's a depression that will make the Dirty Thirties seem like good times by comparison. Millions of people will never work again!"

Instead of religious leaders warning us to prepare to meet our fate, we have economists, columnists and talk-show hosts using these difficult times to preach a message of doom and despair. These seekers after darkness show up in every period of great change, but historically they have found their best audiences at the turn of the centuries, when people expected — and most feared the consequences of — tumultuous upheaval. Are we going to be like the superstitious people of bygone eras and make the silly presumption that the world ends here? Or is something else — something much better — just beginning?

Just look outside your window and you can see that the world is changing. But what is it changing into, and what do these changes mean, in *practical terms,* for the decisions that individuals, companies and governments have to make in their day-to-day lives?

What has been making the headlines and the nighttime newscasts is the bad news — the inevitable turmoil and pain that march in lockstep with each and every transformation — presented as if it were the result of political incompetence, plain bad luck or some international conspiracy (usually a version of the Japanese-are-out-to-destroy-us approach to economic analysis). But what we're not being told is that there is a genuine silver lining underneath the grim layoffs, the plant closings and the bankruptcies. Mighty new industries are rising up to replace the tired old ones.

145

The problem is that the experts charged with explaining our future are still being guided by the beacons of the old economy, which is why their forecasts appear a lot gloomier than they should be. The plain truth is that things change, and always have. In *Shifting Gears,* what I have set out to do is identify what the North American economy has changed into and design a clear road map to the future.

The exhilarating task began more than four years ago with one simple question: What's growing and what's not? After examining in detail hundreds of industries through my consulting firm, Nuala Beck & Associates Inc., it became clear that many of the industries long considered the powerhouses of the economy had actually been in decline for much longer than most people realized. Meanwhile, scores of other industries that were being described as "emerging" and "still too small to really matter" were in fact simply huge.

Once it became clear that these new industries were now North America's mighty engines of growth, the challenge became one of how to measure their strength and influence.

Most of us are much more comfortable in the world we have always known; we are so busy taking care of our day-to-day concerns that we often fail to see change until it has overwhelmed us. Economists are no different. For all their skills at peering ahead, they much prefer spending their time looking back. Change slinks like an unwelcome visitor into their intricately designed computer models, ripping apart comfortable assumptions and carefully crafted sermons.

• • •

But this book is not merely about numbers and trends. Nor is it an academic treatment that describes the theories and relationships at work in the new economy. That will come later. For now, my goal is to lay out a road map that can be read and followed by anyone eager to make sense of the changes affecting all of us, whether we hold in our hands the fate of a giant corporation or simply our own economic futures.

Since I first started talking about my findings about eighteen months ago, the response from business and government at every level has been overwhelming. But it is the response of people whose lives have been so affected by change that has touched me the most. Through them I've learned that economics is about the real world.

Getting the Details

Now that you know the subject, find the answers to these questions. Find the lines that support your answers and note the line numbers.

1 Historically, people preaching messages of doom have found their best audiences

 a) in bygone eras.

 b) at the turn of the centuries.

 c) on the nighttime newscasts.

 d) in difficult times.

 Line(s)

2 Nuala Beck describes what's making the headlines in newspapers and on television newscasts as

 a) what's growing and what's not.

 b) numbers and trends.

 c) apocalyptic visions.

 d) the bad news.

 Line(s)

3 Economic forecasts appear a lot gloomier than they should be because

 a) of plain bad luck.

 b) Nuala Beck & Associates Inc. didn't prepare them.

 c) they are based on computer models.

 d) the experts are guided by the past.

 Line(s)

4 In *Shifting Gears*, Nuala Beck wants to

 a) find a genuine silver lining.

 b) lay out a road map of the economy.

 c) look back at the beacons of the past.

 d) detail hundreds of industries.

 Line(s)

5 The word Nuala Beck uses to describe the task she began more than four years ago is

 a) "overwhelming".

 b) "exhilarating".

 c) "apocalyptic".

 d) "emerging".

 Line(s)

6 Many industries long considered the powerhouses of the economy are

 a) in decline.

 b) emerging.

 c) still too small to matter.

 d) simply huge.

 Line(s)

7 Nuala Beck says she learned economics is about the real world

 a) from the Japanese.

 b) from giant corporations.

 c) from people whose lives have been affected by change.

 d) from business and government at every level.

 Line(s)

Appendix

Irregular Verbs

Base Form	Past Tense	Past Participle	Base Form	Past Tense	Past Participle
	— A —		cling	clung	clung
arise	arose	arisen	come	came	come
awake	awoke	awoken	cost	cost	cost
	— B —		creep	crept	crept
be	was	been	cut	cut	cut
bear	bore	borne *or* born		— D —	
beat	beat	beaten	deal	dealt	dealt
become	became	become	dig	dug	dug
begin	began	begun	do	did	done
bend	bent	bent	draw	drew	drawn
bet	bet	bet	drink	drank	drunk
bid	bid	bid	drive	drove	driven
bind	bound	bound		— E —	
bite	bit	bitten	eat	ate	eaten
bleed	bled	bled		— F —	
blow	blew	blown	fall	fell	fallen
break	broke	broken	feed	fed	fed
breed	bred	bred	feel	felt	felt
bring	brought	brought	fight	fought	fought
broadcast	broadcast	broadcast	find	found	found
build	built	built	flee	fled	fled
burst	burst	burst	fling	flung	flung
buy	bought	bought	fly	flew	flown
	— C —		forbid	forbade *or* forbad	forbidden *or* forbid
cast	cast	cast	forecast	forecast	forecast
catch	caught	caught	foresee	foresaw	foreseen
choose	chose	chosen			

Base Form	Past Tense	Past Participle	Base Form	Past Tense	Past Participle
foretell	foretold	foretold	lose	lost	lost
forget	forgot	forgotten	— M —		
forgive	forgave	forgiven	make	made	made
forsake	forsook	forsaken	mean	meant	meant
forswear	forswore	forsworn	meet	met	met
freeze	froze	frozen	mistake	mistook	mistaken
— G —			misunder-stand	misunder-stood	misunder-stood
get	got	got *or* gotten	— O —		
give	gave	given	overcome	overcame	overcome
go	went	gone	overdo	overdid	overdone
grind	ground	ground	overdraw	overdrew	overdrawn
grow	grew	grown	overtake	overtook	overtaken
— H —			— P —		
hang	hung	hung	pay	paid	paid
have	had	had	put	put	put
hear	heard	heard	— Q —		
hide	hid	hidden	quit	quit	quit
hit	hit	hit	— R —		
hold	held	held	read	read	read
hurt	hurt	hurt	rid	rid	rid
— K —			ride	rode	ridden
keep	kept	kept	ring	rang	rung
know	knew	known	rise	rose	risen
— L —			run	ran	run
lay	laid	laid	— S —		
lead	led	led	say	said	said
leave	left	left	see	saw	seen
lend	lent	lent	seek	sought	sought
let	let	let	sell	sold	sold
lie	lay	lain			

Base Form	Past Tense	Past Participle	Base Form	Past Tense	Past Participle
send	sent	sent	string	strung	strung
set	set	set	strive	strove	striven
shake	shook	shaken	swear	swore	sworn
shed	shed	shed	sweep	swept	swept
shine	shone	shone	swim	swam	swum
shoot	shot	shot	swing	swung	swung
shrink	shrank or shrunk	shrunk		— T —	
shut	shut	shut	take	took	taken
sing	sang	sung	teach	taught	taught
sink	sank	sunk	tear	tore	torn
sit	sat	sat	tell	told	told
slay	slew	slain	think	thought	thought
sleep	slept	slept	throw	threw	thrown
slide	slid	slid	thrust	thrust	thrust
sling	slung	slung		— U —	
slink	slunk	slunk	understand	understood	understood
slit	slit	slit	undo	undid	undone
speak	spoke	spoken		— W —	
speed	sped	sped	wake	woke	woken or waken
spend	spent	spent			
spin	spun	spun	waylay	waylaid	waylaid
spit	spat or spit	spat or spit	wear	wore	worn
split	split	split	weave	wove	woven
spread	spread	spread	weep	wept	wept
spring	sprang	sprung	withhold	withheld	withheld
stand	stood	stood	win	won	won
steal	stole	stolen	wind	wound	wound
stick	stuck	stuck	wring	wrung	wrung
sting	stung	stung	write	wrote	written
stink	stank	stunk			
strike	struck	struck			

Some verbs have both regular and irregular forms:

Base Form	Past Tense	Past Participle	Base Form	Past Tense	Past Participle
burn	burned, burnt	burned, burnt	plead	pleaded, pled	pleaded, pled
dive	dived, dove	dived	prove	proved	proved, proven
dream	dreamed, dreamt	dreamed, dreamt	saw	sawed	sawed, sawn
fit	fitted, fit	fitted, fit	sew	sewed	sewed, sewn
heave	heaved, hove	heaved, hove	show	showed	showed, shown
input	inputted, input	inputted, input	smell	smelled, smelt	smelled, smelt
kneel	kneeled, knelt	kneeled, knelt	spell	spelled, spelt	spelled, spelt
knit	knitted, knit	knitted, knit	spill	spilled, spilt	spilled, spilt
lean	leaned, leant	leaned, leant	spoil	spoiled, spoilt	spoiled, spoilt
leap	leaped, lept	leaped, lept	swell	swelled	swelled, swollen
learn	learned, learnt	learned, learnt	wed	wedded, wed	wedded, wed
light	lighted, lit	lighted, lit	wet	wetted, wet	wetted, wet
mow	mowed	mowed, mown			

Contractions of Auxiliary and Semi-auxiliary Verbs

Full Form	Contracted Form*	With *Not*	Full Form	Contracted Form*	With *Not*
am	'm	——	can	——	can't
is	's	isn't	could	——	couldn't
are	're	aren't	might	——	mightn't
was	——	wasn't	must	——	mustn't
were	——	weren't	should	——	shouldn't
do	——	don't	will	'll	won't
does	——	doesn't	would	'd	wouldn't
did	——	didn't			
have	've	haven't			
has	's	hasn't			
had	'd	hadn't			

* With subject pronouns, noun subjects, *there* and question words.

Personal Pronouns

Subject	Object	Possessive + Noun	Possessive Alone	Reflexive
I	me	my	mine	myself
you	you	your	yours	yourself
he	him	his	his	himself
she	her	her	hers	herself
it	it	its	——	itself
we	us	our	ours	ourselves
you	you	your	yours	yourselves
they	them	their	theirs	themselves

Grammar Index